ARIADNE

F. L. LUCAS

ARIADNE

CAMBRIDGE
AT THE UNIVERSITY PRESS
MCMXXXII

CAMBRIDGE
UNIVERSITY PRESS

University Printing House, Cambridge CB2 8BS, United Kingdom

Published in the United States of America by Cambridge University Press, New York

Cambridge University Press is part of the University of Cambridge.

It furthers the University's mission by disseminating knowledge in the pursuit of education, learning and research at the highest international levels of excellence.

www.cambridge.org
Information on this title: www.cambridge.org/9781107677524

© Cambridge University Press 1932

First published 1932
First paperback edition 2014

A catalogue record for this publication is available from the British Library

ISBN 978-1-107-67752-4 Paperback

To

PRUDENCE

"Pooh!—from a lover!—this moth-eaten tale!
What a superannuated nightingale—
A thing three thousand years old at the least!
You know I'm rather younger! What a feast
Fit for one's grandmother, warranted to bring
Slumbers as sound as the *Idylls of the King*!
Why *will* you waste your—well, we will not say
'Talents'—your time, on such worn-out child's-
       play?"
"Because I want to." "But you're living *now*."
"Alas!" "*That's* gallant!" "Foolish, you know how
I prize my happiness. But all the same,
If I turn backwards, too, to times less tame,
Is that so idle? Little nymph, confess!—
You whom the Muses, like the Graces, bless,
Whose young lips laugh in Greek—think you as great
King Xerxes' as King Agamemnon's fate
On the stage of Aeschylus? If Horace wrote
Of his own day, and not of things remote,
Have men less eagerly heard Virgil tell
How a thousand years before him Ilium fell?

Is Milton less than Pope? Is there a hue
(Except those eyes) more lovely than the blue
Of distance—far away and long ago—
Where dwells *la princesse lointaine?* "Distance? Oh!
So charming, is it? I'll keep mine and be
Remote as ten princesses. You shall see!"
"Be serious, you imp. Both worlds are true,
The past and Ariadne, now and you—
Both I must have." "Ah, but in poetry
Newness is now the fashion—verse must be
'Modern' or nothing." "Often both! What's great
No one can know till it *is* out of date."
"An epigram!" "Then, frivolous thing, who need
Write of his age, or for it, to succeed?
And such an age as this!—when verse is grown
The public place where epileptics moan,
Dragging their sores like Lazarus to the gate
For curs to lick, and fools to contemplate;
The stage for eunuchs imitating Donne
Whose periwinkle minds in circles run,
Blind, bloodless, tasteless, tortuous!—" "Ho, what
    rage!
Who's peevish! Well, visit your vanished age,
Since you prefer being dead—you can't *live* there."
"Not there alone. The past is everywhere,
Entwined with all our present—each new breath

viii

Of air we breathe, is old as Life and Death."
"But write of what you know." "The wild Greek
    hills,
And war, and death, and that worse pain that kills
Love in two hearts grown bitter—these I know,
They were little changed three thousand years ago;
Love least of all, that Siren who betrays
Men's hearts, half god, half beast—that Sphinx who
    lays
Her eternal riddle: 'Change, or constancy?
The One, or Many? Bound, or gaily free?'"
"What! Have you *doubts*! Of constancy! To *me*!
But this grows more interesting." "Egotist!
It's growing clear enough why you insist
On 'modern' subjects. *You* would be my theme,
Not Ariadne?" "Ah, at last, a gleam
Of common sense. Yes, foolish, I should be
Your subject." "O twice foolish, not to see
You are!—dear hands that held the saving clue
To that dark labyrinth I wandered through
So hopelessly. And whose eyes were they, shone
Between my labouring lines to lead them on?
Without the gift of yours, O my delight,
How had your lover found the heart to write?"
"My heart, indeed!—and all the world to know it!
I lost my head, to give it to a poet!"

I

δίζησθαι δὲ φιλαγλάους Ἀθάνας.

Bacchylides.

Set out for Athens, land that loves the light.

I

Twice, since the dawn, far down the Athenian plain
Had stormed the long white lances of the rain,
While the sword-blades of the lightning, jag on jag,
Plunged and replunged from crag to bellowing crag
High up Hymettus. Now once more the gloom
Cracked into blue, and towering from his tomb
The sun flashed out across the Attic land.
And now by twos and threes on every hand,
From shelter of dripping thatch or smoke-hung door,
The men of Athens slowly flocked once more
To the place of their assembly. Fair as Heaven
About them lay the land their gods had given:
Wrecks of the storm, along Hymettus hill
Slow wisps of silver vapour floated still;
Sharp from the east Pentelicus arose,
Crowned now anew with sun-resplendent snows;
While, to the north, the black bulk of Parnes
Scowled and trod down the mists that clutched his knees.
Yet not to the hills men looked, but where the sea
Swung westward to the Isthmus. Merrily
Its shimmering dance of waters, far away,
Laughed: but in those dumb eyes no laughter lay,

Till, like a gust through rustling barley, swept
A shudder through them—round the headland crept
A blackened galley with a blackened sail.
Then women's voices rose in one wild wail,
And red young lips breathed faster, and bearded
    cheeks grew pale.
So, huddled, helpless, sheep on the mountain-side
Forth from the forest watch the grey wolf glide.
But sudden a trumpet pealed. Men turned. There came,
Girt with his guards (yet no voice hailed his name),
Aegeus the king; a king, but tottering, ill,
A broken body with a breaking will.
Alone in that waxen mask the brown eyes burned
With a flicker of bright fever, as they turned
From face to face, peering what lay behind,
Afraid to see, yet fearing to be blind;
As one whose morrow holds no gift but death,
No gift to-day, except its gift of breath,
Sweet still, although so bitter. By his side,
Armed, his tall nephews paced in their glittering pride,
Hard faces eyeing his with sneer or frown—
"Shall Death, or we, first drag this dotard down?"—
And last, amidst a hiss of whispered hate,
With head held high and lordly-striding gait,
Broad in the shoulders, weirdly pinched at waist
(Like some huge hornet), dark-skinned, hairless-faced,

4

The stranger come last night from overseas.
To his throne King Aegeus stumbled; on his knees
His old hound laid its grizzled head and whined—
Little love else he found there. Grim, resigned,
All Athens stood, while the hoarse heralds cried
For "Silence!" through their silence. Shame and pride
Stung him—he started up, their king again,
A king though conquered, a king though bowed
    with pain,
His country beaten. Ah, vain words—once more
His eyes met that grim stranger, then the shore,
And that black hull in far Phalerum bay—
He gnawed his hand, he bowed his head away.
As the shrieking hare that feels the hounds' hot
    breath
Ruffle her fur, and knows now "This is death,"
Yet plies her cunning, strains her breaking will,
Doubles and twists to live one moment still;
So sought those hunted eyes one instant's grace.
He bit his lip, then paused—with altered face,
And look half childish cunning and half shame,
"Men of Athens," he began "last night there came
News from the Isthmus—news of murder done—
Great Sciron, lord of Megara, Pylas' son,
My sister's husband, slain by a hand unknown,
Some vagrant from the Southland, young, alone,

5

Fled, they say, none knows whither. For that blood shed
We set a price upon the slayer's head—
Its weight in silver. Therefore, if any here
Knows more, speak out!" Around him, far and near,
Eyes opened wider, sudden breaths were drawn,
Hope gleamed an instant—could they be met this morn
Only for that? But no—the stranger there!—
Grey grew their faces with the old despair,
As they watched upon those cold thin lips the while
Hover the glimmer of a frozen smile.
The King sank back: but from the crowd there cried
An old priest robed in white, lank, ferret-eyed,
With a shrill, insolent voice: "Dead? Dead indeed!—
Lord Sciron died two days since. Little need
To cry that news in Athens. I have heard
A stranger thing." He lingered on the word,
Drinking their wonder, while the old king frowned
And looked away. But proudly staring round,
Flapping gaunt arms, the priest cried "Late last night
I had word from Eleusis. God does right!—
What wrongs men do, they too shall undergo;
Justice at last comes home, though halt her feet and slow.
High though kings sit, and all the kin of kings,
Puffed up with pride, she ends their gloryings;
He that hurled strangers from that headland's brow
By Megara, himself is fallen now.

So ended Sciron. Now another lord,
King Kerkyon of Eleusis, the Abhorred,
Who has made all comers wrestle a fall with him
These ten years past, and wrenched them limb from limb
Until they died—ay, at Demeter's feast
Down Her own steps he flung Demeter's priest,
My cousin"—striding from behind the throne
The tallest of the princes, Agrion
The son of Pallas, gripped him, growling "Fool,
That was a crime indeed! Go!—back to school,
Old insolence, and learn before too late,
Before you share your holy cousin's fate,
Princes have ears as sharp as priests have tongues to prate!
Out with your news! How fares my stout old friend
King Kerkyon?—and long may Heaven send
Strangers in plenty for his exercise!"
But, staggering back, the priest with narrowed eyes
Hissed out "My prince, the king you love so well
Fares as he should—along the road to Hell!"
Then to the King—"'Slain by a hand unknown,
A vagrant from the Southland, young, alone'—
And he comes, they say, towards Athens!" Low he
    bowed
With a harsh laugh, then vanished in the crowd,
That buzzed like bees at swarming. Furiously
Once more Prince Agrion bade the heralds cry

For silence, and upraised his hand, and said:
"A double price upon this stranger's head,
Twice its full weight in silver. Who knows more?"
Then a broad sailor from Phalerum shore
Thrust up a sea-tanned arm—"Why, this might be
The youth we saw six days back, by the sea
At Epidaurus. Fair-haired, tall, and slim—
And bound for Athens! We remembered him;
For we would have given him passage, sure and swift,
By sea—but he, he smiled away our gift.
We said 'So afraid of drowning? Safer far
The maddest sea than the road by Megara.'
'Therefore' said he 'by Megara I go';
And gaily laughed, and stood and watched us row
Out towards Methana. A cloak of Thessaly
He had—and a crimson tunic. Good to see
Flash on his golden head the burnished brass
Of his helm of Lacedaemon. Up the pass
We watched it twinkling. Pity it was, we thought,
So brave a lad should go to death self-sought.
But three days after, as by chance we lay
For water at Aegina, we heard say
Sinnis the Pinetree-bender, that for years
Has skulked above the Isthmus—he that tears
Travellers in sunder 'twixt two bended trees—
Had been found served as he had served all these,

8

Clean severed as a pippin! Judge the rest—
Was this same lad belike King Kerkyon's guest,
That broke his heart for kindness?" Then the Prince—
"No jesting, fellow! Heard you then or since
Whence came this stranger? Where his home had been?"
"He told us that himself. In wild Troezene."
Catching the silver tossed him, jauntily
The sailor turned. But out across the sea
King Aegeus stared, where fifty miles away,
Beyond the blue horn of Aegina, lay
The dim peaks of Troezene. Along their brow
This morning's storm was trailing darkness now.
High in the west towered that huge thundercloud,
A mountain o'er the mountains: changeless, proud,
Its sun-bright summits shone like driven snow,
Like sheer black crags its cloud-banks loured below,
While through their rifted gloom the deathly dance
Of lightning flickered. But the old King's glance
Had softened now to sadness. Through his tears
He saw on far Troezene sunlight of other years.
But harshly on his trance a strange voice broke,
Husky, uncouth. From that dear dream he woke
And drew his hand across his brow and sighed—
A peasant stood there. Greedily he eyed
The sailor pouching up his silver piece;
As he spoke, one gnarled hand twitched the greasy fleece

9

That wrapped his shoulders, and one long-clawed palm
He waved before him—"Listen, Lord. My farm
Lies there by Corydallus, up the hill—
A cursed place, iron land it is to till,
Wind-nipped in winter, scorched in summertime,
All thorns and rocks that scarce a goat could climb.
Still, mine had climbed. I hunted them last night,
High up Aegaleus. In the grey twilight
Grim lay the glen beyond. Then, up its track,
I saw move, far away, one dot of black.
'A stranger' thought I. 'Sure, this is no hour
To stray among these hills.' Then from the Tower
Far up the glen, where we folk fear to go,
Lest we meet Him—He is not good to know—
He came. High up I watched. I saw them meet—
Sure, He was bidding the stranger rest and eat;
For in they went. Not once nor twice before
Guests have I seen that entered, but none that left
          that door."
Dog-toothed, he chuckled: but King Aegeus groaned—
"Is it come to this? O God, that I had died
Before the day that on a mountainside
Three hours from Athens things like this could be—
And I a king, this my authority!
What do you whisper? Why was I never told?
Ah, better buried deep than thus grown old,

None round my throne but the sons of riot and dance."
Silent the princes grew beneath his glance,
Only their eyes encountered, smiling scorn.
But laughing Macareus, the youngest-born,
Cried "On with your tale, old prick-louse! What
    came next?"
But the peasant scratched his grizzled head, perplexed
Like a mule between two pastures, looking now
To the King, now to the Princes, all his brow
Puckered with pondering where the kingdom lay,
Misdoubting all his pains might miss their pay.
Then bending low to Agrion he said
"I found my goats. A weary chase they led—"
"Plague on your goats" the Prince cried, with his hand
Upraised to strike, "and plague upon your land!
Have done!" The old man cringed—"My lord, to-day
I rose ere light—for 'tis a weary way
To market. Said my wife 'Up, slug-a-bed,
You have lain too long! Look how the dawn grows
    red.'
I wondered 'twas so late. I took the road.
But lo! good lord, it was the north that glowed!—
The east lay dark as death. I grew afraid—
Thought I 'They have fired the beacon. 'Tis a raid
Across Parnes? Or the Cretan fleet once more?
Or is King Eurystheus riding out to war

From Mycenae the Golden?' Up the hill
I climbed to look, and lo! no beacon-fire,
But in the glen beyond, like some tall pyre
At a king's burial, the Tower burned,
With a great red beard of flame that tossed and
    turned
In the night-wind. I scrambled down. There stood,
Glaring in that mad light as red as blood,
One with a bare blade glittering in his hand,
Waiting. Then I began to understand—
It was the stranger—seemed he did not like
His lodging. All at once, I saw him strike
At something in the door; and with a yell
From the red-hot roof two others leapt and fell,
And lay not moving. Just as when ere now
I have found a wasps' nest hanging on a bough
At home, and put red iron to it, and stood
Waiting to smash the stragglers of the brood;
Or with the rats at threshing—ah good lord,
Be patient—I have done. He sheathed his sword
Slowly, and all lay silent, save the roar
Of long flames licking up from floor to floor,
And crackling through the ivy. Up the sky
The dawn was creeping now, and crouched close by
I could see the stranger clearly—I could see
A youth in a crimson tunic!—sure, 'twas he!"

Amid the hush, while all men held their breath,
"Fellow," said Aegeus "he that died this death,
The Tower's lord—you have not said his name."
Across that wizened face the old dread came;
He whispered low "Procrustes! Some men said,
That dared to talk, he kept a wondrous bed."
Darkly he leered; then the King's marshal laid
Silver across his gaping palm. He weighed
The three bright pieces with a sneering look.
The marshal pushed him—"Go!" But nothing shook
That tight-lipped mouth. "Remember, lord," he said
The price you promised for the stranger's head—
Double its weight." Fierce laughed Prince Agrion—
"Yes, and as well the full weight of your own
(And that is light enough) the day you bring
This murderer of men to the presence of the King,
Living or dead. Now throw the fellow hence!"
He turned. But shouting "Then my recompense!"
The old man leapt on one that quietly stood
Three paces off, and tore the traveller's hood
With one hand from his head, and snatched aside
His mantle with the other, as he cried—
"The lad with the crimson tunic! Ah, ye thought
Old Theron a poor fool—now are ye taught?
I dogged his heels to Athens—yes, this day!
Justice, Lord King! Is not the price to pay?"

For thirty breathless heart-beats every tongue
Was hushed—till suddenly the seaman flung
His cap to Heaven and cried "It is, by God!
Brave lad! Brave lad!" But with an angry nod
To the captain of the guard Prince Agrion signed
"Seize him!" Alone before them all, half-blind
With sudden sunlight, for an instant there
A girl's flush crimsoned that young face laid bare.
Then, as he saw their dumb mouths gaping round,
Loud through that multitude without a sound
His laughter rang—so young, so blithe, so gay
It brought a smile to faces worn and grey
And care from hearts that heard it for an instant
    dropped away—
As though all sorrow, all life's bitter truth
Turned to a dream before the laugh of youth.
But wilder grew the look in Aegeus' eyes,
Lit with a sudden, passionate surmise.
That laughter!—from so far it reached his ears,
From fifty miles away, and twenty years.
How could it be? Yet in the lower lip
That curve; those clear grey eyes that from his ship
In a yet lovelier face—how long ago!—
He had seen fixed on his, while to and fro
The sea-wind tossed about them curls of gold
Just such as these—in a flash the past unrolled,

Before his eyes the rock-bound harbour lay,
The plunging ship, the rain, the shrieking spray,
That kerchieft head bent sideways to the gale,
That long-forsaken face, so brave and pale,
Smiling farewell to him—he looked up. Lo,
With levelled spears his guards closed round their foe.
Out flashed the stranger's sword and with one spring
Clean through their line he leapt before the King,
Crying "To you I yield, no lesser lord";
Then with a gay, shy smile held out his sword,
Hilt foremost. It was wrought of ivory,
Yellow with years; but marvellous yet to see
How down that blade of doom with stony eyes
Two couchant Sphinxes gazed, calm, changeless,
    wise,
On the brief lives and barren deaths of men.
But when the old King's eyes fell on it, then
With one wild cry "My son, my son, my son!"
His white locks mingled with that golden head.
But like metal in a furnace, dusky-red
Grew Agrion's face. He flung one warning look
Back to his brothers; then, in a voice that shook
With anger, cried "Have done! All Athens waits,
Murder at home, the Cretan at our gates.
We need, not long-lost bastards found again,
But justice on the slayer for the slain."

15

But Aegeus turned to the people—"Zeus be praised—
Praise Him, O men of Athens, who has raised
A new hope for Erechtheus' race once more.
This is the son of Aethra, whom she bore
In far Troezene, these twenty years agone—
Aethra, the child of Pittheus, Pelops' son
And Atreus' brother; of that house whose fame
Bears through all earth the great Achaean name.
Look, for the lost is found, the dead arise,
My son smiles on me with his mother's eyes."
Then Sthenelus, son of Pallas, shouted loud
"Proof, in God's name, what proof?" But Aegeus
    bowed
His head in sadness—"Then, to win my throne
I left my love; with her, beneath a stone
Such as few else could lift—how long, how long
Since once these shrunk and withered arms were
    strong!—
This sword with the carven Sphinxes, for a sign
That if she bore a son, her son was mine,
True heir, though I should perish, of Erechtheus'
    ancient line.
I won my kingdom, but I broke my word.
A new face witched me, and a new love stirred
My heart to other thoughts than of Troezene,
My love forsaken and my child unseen.

A year passed. Then I sent. Her answer said
My child had been a daughter, and was dead—
Dead as her love, dead as the memory
Of days so sweet to have, so swift to flee.
I did not doubt. I fought but to forget,
Through those wild years of war. What help to fret
For things long done? I did not guess, beguiled,
That one who had lost her lover, might lie to keep
    her child."
Then jeered a son of Pallas "Hers. But his?
Know you—knows he—knows any—who his own
    father is?"
But the old King shook his head—"Too well, I know
That heart once mine." But whispering to and fro
Among the Pallantids Prince Agrion passed,
Then to the captain of the guard he cast
One stealthy look, before he shouted "Hear,
Before too late, King Aegeus. Year on year
We have endured you and your reckless reign,
Our land misgoverned and our people slain.
You have brought the Cretan on us; you have wed
That harlot from the Eastland, you have bred
One son by her—" He pointed as he spoke
Towards the palace, while a low growl woke
Among the crowd. "And now, behold, there starts
Out of the earth, to gladden all our hearts,

This bastard from Troezene! Long, all too long
We sons of Pallas have been loth to wrong
Our father's brother. But we will not see
The crown that is our right, by trickery
Shuffled to others. On this stranger's head
Lies blood of ours: his blood is ours to shed.
Mark well my word, King Aegeus. Justly fill
Your judgment-seat—or yield to one that will!"
Then shouting round him rallied, face to face
With Aegeus, those tall sons of Pallas' race,
And all their followers, from Pallene's plain,
From Oa and from Erchia, from the fane
Of Artemis by Brauron, from the sea
That bathes the olives' feet at Prasiae.
And next, at Agrion's beck, the King's own spears
Forsook the King—his own fierce mountaineers
From Rhamnus and the March of Marathon.
Grimly all Athens watched while sire and son
Were left there standing side by side, alone.
Then Aegeus bowed his white head with a groan,
Too proud, too desperate, to cry for aid—
His reign was ended, and his part was played.
But from those threatening spears the young man turned
To face his father's people. Crimson burned
Upon his cheeks pity and rage and shame
For the old man's sake; a sob, but no words, came

From his dry lips; he felt fixed on him there,
As he strove to speak, the crowd's cold, curious stare.
Close on his left he saw the smiling sneer
On Agrion's face; before him, blue and clear,
The mountains of Troezene beyond the bay,
The hills of home—how far, how far they lay,
With all he loved! Then rose up, stern and sweet,
The eyes of Aethra—he heard her voice repeat
His name—with head thrown back, "Is this my home,"
He cried "you men of Athens? Must I come
Thus to my father and my fatherland?
Ah if you knew how often I would stand
Looking towards Athens seaward from Troezene,
These six years—since the day I was fourteen!
That eve my mother led me up the hill
Of our Acropolis; like sleep—so still—
Lay grey Troezene, and then the sunset sea,
And then the girdling land's immensity
From Mount Parnassus to Cape Sunium.
'Theseus,' she said 'you know not whence you come.
Yours is another city, nobler-planned,
Than this Troezene, this little, well-loved land.
Look—where across the sea the sun's last glow
Purples one peak, Hymettus; and below
Glitters a speck of white—there stand the walls
Your fathers built, the burg the wide earth calls

"Athens." You too, my son, shall pass its gate
One day; and find your fortune, or your fate.'
O men of Athens, from that hour there seemed
But one place in the world. All day I dreamed
Of your fair Athens, that was mine as well,
Of this fair Athens where I too should dwell:
From lips of blind old men or bent old wives
I learned the legends of your land—the lives
Men lived, or lost, that Athens through all earth
Might stand remembered—all the mystic birth
Of old Erechtheus—how his daughters gave
Youth that had known no lover's kiss, to save
Their country from the Thracian—then the tale
Of Procris, and of Procne, and the wail
For Itys dead, and Oreithyia lost.
Never a day since then but these eyes crossed
The sea to seek you; sad, when the blinding rain
Blotted you out, gay when the sun again
Lit white your wall. But still I did not know
Who was my father; till, ten days ago,
My mother woke me. Up the dewy wood
Through the mists of dawn we climbed, until she stood
Before a great grey boulder, saying, 'Son,
Here lies your heritage. My part is done.'
She wept. I heaved it back—and lo, the sword!
But when she told me that my sire was lord

Of Athens—then, I thought my heart would break
With pride, and joy, and shame for my own sake—
Since how could I deserve it? So I came
By land, in hope to show I should not shame,
Not wholly shame my race. What trials I met
Ye know. But now—would God I had never set
Foot in this land, would I had never seen
The gate of Athens, but in grey Troezene
Lived on, and wooed a wife, and seen my race
Grow round her knees, and found my resting-place
In calm old age, nor learnt how nobler dreams
Cheat, and What Is makes mock of poor What Seems.
For what is here?—my father made your slave;
You, slaves to others; and the deeds I gave
To Athens, called my crime!—the foes I foiled,
The slaughterers slaughtered and the spoilers spoiled—
Their guiltless blood, it seems, cries from the ground!
Think you I came here greedy to be crowned?
No, no, not that—I came on fire to find
The father, and the country, that—O blind!—
I had dreamed of all those years. Yet who are these
That bawl of 'rights' and 'birthrights' at their ease?
Are you their beasts? To be sold from hand to hand—
Bequeathed like chattels—parcelled out, like land?
You have a king—why brawl these tongues to-day,
Whom ye shall crown hereafter? Who shall say

'Mine are ye next'? They told me in Troezene
You held heads high in Athens, that your Queen
Was She of the Gorgon-Shield, who kneels to none
Save the Lord of all Earth and Heaven, Cronus' son.
Have I not seen, yonder across the hills,
The rich Mycenae, where Eurystheus fills
With toll and tribute wrung from land and sea
The glittering darkness of his treasury?—
With ivory gleam his walls, with bronze his doors,
Great bulls stalk through his pastures, grain heaps
        his threshing-floors—
'Yet what of these?' thought I. 'Could I be proud
To rule this whispering people, cringing, cowed?
Better by far that barren Attic earth
Where men speak freely; where men boast their
        worth
From the greatness of the city, not the house, that
        gave them birth.'
Was this all false? Are ye no longer free
As in old days, race of Erechtheidae?
Why, then, farewell. I will go my way alone
To find, or found, some city of my own."
He turned. "Farewell too," said he with a sigh
"My father." But like some black rookery
That sees the woodman come—a storm of wings
Whirls into whirring flight, the whole wood rings

While the wild discord of ten thousand throats,
Out-bawling each its fellow, hoarsely floats
Up the blue peace of Heaven; so at once
Rose the fierce shouting—"Down with Pallas' sons!"—
"Long live Prince Theseus!"—"Theseus for our Lord!"
Then the Pallantids paled, without a word
Watching each other. Only Agrion
Strode forward, hand upraised. A jagged stone
Struck full upon his mouth—down his dark beard
The blood dripped red—he heard a voice that jeered,
Caught up a spear and flung. Whizzing, it sped
Between the grey King and the golden head
Of Theseus. Then, with one wild howl of hate
A storm of stones came hurled in answer—straight
Men tore their mantles from them; shepherd-boys
Whipped out their slings; above, with a wild noise
Of wailing, women on the housetops threw
Tiles wrenched up from their places—now there flew,
As men found arms, things deadlier, shaft and spear;
As, when towards harvest sultry grows the year
And in the coppery dusk the low clouds loom
Drowsily darkening—sudden from the gloom
The thunder growls, then leaps the great round rain,
Then the first hailstones—in a flash the plain
Is blind with one white whirl of hurtling hail,
While corn and vine, as though beneath a flail,

23

Go to the ground before it. So that day
The levies of the Pallantids gave way,
The spearmen of the King forgot the gold
Of Agrion, the faith that they had sold,
Before the people's rage—dropped spears and ran.
Only the princes, rallying man to man,
Hacked their way through that tumult to the gate
Leaving four fallen brethren to their fate—
(There Macareus lay still, in his young grace,
A smile upon his happy, lifeless face)—
And sprang to horse and spurred their smoking way
Back to Pallene. But Theseus bade stay
The chase, and called the commons back to fill
Once more their assembly on Athene's Hill.
Once more they gathered, a changed people now—
That nameless dread had lifted from each brow—
Panting and laughing. But as Aegeus rose,
Forth strode the dark-skinned stranger. Lurking close
Behind the throne, yet silent in the shade
Of Athene's temple-columns, while there swayed
Backwards and forwards all the chance and change
Of that wild morning, his cold arrogance
Had watched it all, unmoving, careless, calm
As a rich man that watches on his farm
His poor churls sweat to dig and ditch and drain
Under the whistling lash of wind and rain,

Warm in his mantle. Now with herald's staff
Held high he came, and round him every laugh
Died—with harsh accent and outlandish tongue
"Lord King," said he "this child's-play lasts too long,
Trick me no longer. On another's head
Though you set the price of blood, for blood you shed
The price is still to pay. Let the lots be drawn.
The wind stands fair. The Black Ship sails at dawn.
Therefore, King Aegeus, see I have my freight;
The Lord of Cnossus has not learned to wait."
Turning he stalked away. Then Theseus cried
"Who is this insolent"—but the King, wild-eyed,
Clapped hand across his mouth, and whispered "Son,
No word, in God's name, till this hour is done!
Then you shall hear—God give me strength to tell!
Only keep silence now; and keep it well."
An urn was brought, dead-black. Then sadly came
A scribe, and from a roll read name by name;
For each the grey-haired King, with hand that shook,
Drew from the urn and held for all to look
A single bean; then dropped it in a bowl,
Till soon a white pile gleamed there. Down the scroll,
Name after name, that voice with its dull drone
Read, while the clicking lots fell one by one
And Theseus wondered at those haggard eyes,
Those moistened lips, those little smothered cries

Of joy, as a name passed by. In doubt, his glance
Turned to the King; the King stared in a trance;
Then to the stranger—sea-ward, far away
Those black eyes wandered, dreaming of the day
He should see home and lie once more at ease
In Cnossus, under his own cypress-trees.
Then a mad shriek—and Theseus' gaze leapt back:
High in King Aegeus' hand a bean showed black.
Then from the crowd with sobbing and lament
A little band crept forth; and onward went
That voice relentless reading down the roll,
While ever and again some anguished soul
Shrieked out, and a group of mourners went their way,
Till all was ended. Like a load it lay
On Theseus' heart to see eyes red and dim
With weeping, turned so piteously to him
In looks of half-crazed hope, half-dazed despair.
They scattered. Noon flamed down. Beneath its glare
Mistier grew the mirror of the sea,
Hazy the hills. Sleep of eternity
Seemed brooding on their wrinkled heads of stone,
While like a fierce, low lullaby the drone
Of insects left the stillness yet more still.
White Athens slept, and Lycabettus hill,
Colonus with its groves of silver-grey,
The roads that wound across the hills away.

So quiet the world was grown, in that deep peace
It seemed man's ancient sorrow too must cease,
Even his grief find rest, even his pain release.
   But through his palace-porch the old King led,
Through an empty court, to a hall with embers dead.
Marble its floor, marble its pillars were,
Yet its white stillness seemed but bleak and bare
To eyes that had seen Mycenae—fair, but cold,
Work of a land more rich in stone than gold,
In wit than wealth. Yet here and there were hung
Strange broideries where writhing dragons flung
Coils of bright gold about blue-branching trees,
Mixed with weird shapes and mystic phantasies,
With many an unknown bird and monstrous beast
Bred of the tangled dreaming of the East.
Strange perfumes steeped the air, and still it seemed
As if there some dark presence sat and dreamed,
As if with ancient evil those woven figures teemed.
Yet, as the threshold rang beneath their tread,
Only a lizard, swift as a shadow, fled.
King Aegeus called. Two old slaves limped to bring
The noontide meal. Fond and yet sad, the King,
Eager and yet afraid, gazed on his son,
If son it could be—asked of his deeds late done;
And then, more faintly, of far-off Troezene;
Not naming Aethra. Yet, unnamed, unseen,

27

She came between them there: for one, a face
Known always, loved so well in its worn grace,
He scarce could dream it young; for one, a bride
Bright with the beauty that long since had died
Waiting, far off, through twenty wasted years—
How swiftly fled! He felt himself the same,
Weaker, yet hardly changed—and lo! there came
One that was nothing when those years began,
Not even a span-long infant; now a man,
A slayer of men!—he shrank from that young gaze
Risen to judgment on his squandered days.
"My son," he cried "I know your hidden thought—
You have not found the father that you sought;
Ah, well I know. You dreamed of a king grown old
Amid his people's blessings—and behold,
(Yes, yours the word) you find their 'slave' instead,
One that forsook your mother." With bowed head
Sat Theseus. Sadly, the old man went on
"How strange, how strange the thing that is done
        and gone,
Past God's own power to undo; past man's wit,
When he looks back, himself to fathom it!
For I loved Aethra—O learn this, my son,
This lesson I can teach; the only one—
I have paid to learn it. Think not true love grows
Through all the world, as the wild poppy blows

Red on a thousand fields, a thousand hills.
Youth thinks it so—to find just as it wills
The red bloom of desire in every lane,
Easy to pluck, to drop, to find again.
Youth does not know." The old man smiled to see
His son's eyes dreamy now with memory;
With memory of the Isthmus—that grim glen
Where he had slain the Pine-bender—and then
A rustle in the thicket, two brown eyes
Like a scared fawn's, and sweet low piteous cries,
As he dragged forth his quarry, a slim maid
Shy as a Dryad in a woodland glade,
Trembling and sobbing for her father's fate.
Sweet that had been, so sweet, as night grew late,
Her young head pillowed on him, while her hair
Caressed his lips, and lying he watched the Bear,
Through the black fir-tops, prowling round the
        Pole;
So sweet, he felt he could forget his goal
And all the call of Athens, just to stay
There in the greenwood with her. Then the day
Returning shook him from that idle dream.
But still he could see her standing by the stream
At the wood's edge where they parted—those
        brown eyes
Watching him go, with wistful, dumb surprise.

Ah, if again—but no, the world was wide,
No more, no more would they sleep side by side.
His wandering thoughts flew back. With smile and sigh
"Such loves are sweet," said Aegeus "but they die.
They are not love, although men call them so;
Love is less light to come, less light to go;
Like that strange herb no human hand has sown,
Moly, the gift of Gods, and Gods alone.
Ah Theseus, if They give you what They gave
Me—such a heart, so strong, so loyal, so brave
As bred you in Troezene—remember then,
Though I am dust long, long forgot of men,
No words of mine but these—come what come may,
Fling all you have, but not that love, away.
Think not the Gods who gave, will give again
What most men pray to have but once in vain.
That was my folly—" Suddenly, "The Queen!"
Whispered a slave. There, watching them unseen
She stood. But Theseus reddened angrily—
Set in the seat of Aethra, who was she?
That very step was Aethra's, that tall grace—
His heart stood still to see it. But her face—
Ah, that was other!—fair, not as flesh is fair,
But like a mask of metal. Jet her hair,
But time had marred and crime had scarred that brow
Beneath its whited youth. Yet even now

It kept a haggard splendour in decay,
Like some gaunt, lonely tower, where queens
   once lay,
Turned to a den of robbers. By her side
There skipped her little son, brown, beady-eyed.
Like a sword her glance searched Theseus—"Fair
   of face!"
She cried with a smile to Aegeus. "Like his race—
Fair are you all—and false! So Jason looked."
Smiling she said it; yet her smile grew crooked.
But Theseus knit his forehead at the name:
Back to his thought the taunt of Agrion came—
"That harlot from the Eastland." Could this be,
This, the bright heroine—O mockery!—
The magic Princess of the Colchian shore,
Of whom his nurse had told him, o'er and o'er;
Whose story his own childhood used to play;
Whose glamour witched his boyish heart away!—
This, Jason's love, who won for him the Fleece
And up wild Ister fled with him to Greece!
He had dreamed her dead, dust of a bygone age,
A queen of memory. But dark with rage
At sight of his blank face she cried "In truth
We live too long, King Aegeus! See how youth
Gapes with wide eyes of innocence when it hears
Names that the whole earth rang with, in the years

When we were young. Ah God, to live to see
Argo forgot, forgot the Minyae!
Lies your Troezene so hid, so shut away
From the wide world, you never heard men say
Medea, daughter of Aeetes, sat
By Aegeus—Queen in Athens! But of that
No more—I too knew not that there had been
One Theseus, son of Aegeus, in Troezene."
(Darkly she smiled.) "But welcome now, though late.
No quarrel, Theseus! I am sick of hate.
Enough that the dead is living, the lost is found.
Taste of my loving-cup! Therein be drowned
All jealousy, all bitterness be blind."
She took a gold cup from a slave behind
And stretched it out to him. Again her eyes
Met him, with all their brooding memories—
The sorceries of the East, the secret things
Muttered by Magian priests to Chaldee kings,
Her own dark spells, her own red deeds were there,
Absyrtus' blood, Creusa's blazing hair.
Her mouth smiled fawning, but her glance gleamed cold,
As awful and unalterable to behold
As a tarn no winds can waken where it fills
Some hollow in the black heart of the hills.
"Lady," he said "fear not—your fame is blown
Through all Troezene. But must I drink alone?—

Shall both not taste this cup that binds us one?
Pledge me your love, as to a second son."
Slowly she shook her head—"I drink no wine."
He scanned her face—those dark eyes gave no sign.
Doubting, he raised the cup. She watched. He smiled
And laid it to the red mouth of her child—
"Taste, little brother." She struck his hand aside,
"He is too young—he drinks no wine" she cried.
"Nor I" said Theseus, smiling. But the King
Went white—"You witch, what means this paltering?
Drink!—or they hurl you headlong from the wall."
No word she spoke, but flung far down the hall
The gold cup, jangling on the marble floor;
Then turned to bay, one arm outstretched before
Her whimpering child. Then at her own fireside
By her own husband's hand she would have died,
If Theseus had not flung himself between
And caught the old man's wrist—"Have we not seen
Bloodshed enough this day? Let go, let go,
Let the Gods judge her!—They have made her so,
And man's unkindness. Let her sail home again,
Back to her East. I am too sick of pain
And blood and slaughter. Is there no end? Six days—
Six days of death!" But with dark eyes ablaze,
"O fool," she hissed "O fool, to fling aside,
For a day's upstart, me you have known and tried

These thirteen years! I came, a fugitive—
You saved me. What repayment could I give?—
Myself! Have I not given? Then an heir?
Have I not served you? In your worst despair,
Conquered abroad, at home your people's hate,
Who else stood firm beside you? To your gate
There comes this beardless vagabond, this 'son,'
Loathing you in his heart for wrongs long done
His mother—one that will only count how slow
The days, till you are safely buried—lo!
You weep upon his neck!—have we no child?
So Jason too betrayed me! Twice beguiled!
Such is Greek faith! Such is Greek loyalty!
Come, Medus, come, my child. Ah yet, maybe,
Our race one day shall pay with death and shame
This land that hunts us hence—with sword and flame,
Until men's hearts on their own hearthstones hiss
From Marathon to sea-girt Salamis.
And you, my prince, who draw so bold a breath,
Grow not too proud. A quiet and easy death
You would have died, two days hence. Triumph not yet,
Lest the day come when, groaning, you regret
You died not now. This people loves you—wait,
Darling of Athens, till you feel their hate!"

     She turned and left them; while the young man leant
Against a pillar, with his head down-bent

34

Moodily staring at the ashes there
On the dead hearth, that with blind gusts of air
Rustled and clicked and whirled in eddying rings
Like a ghostly puppet-show's grey flutterings.
Sadly his father watched the brooding face
That had laughed so gaily in the market-place
An hour ago. "Is life in the world like this
Always?" he said. "So full of things amiss,
Of hate and treachery? High up the hills
Lurked Death—but not this air that chokes and kills;
They were less lonely than these cold walls seem,
Those eyes that make my dreams fade like a dream.
This city stifles me—ah God, once more
To hear the wind across the forest roar,
Alone, alone!" He looked up longingly,
Up through the roofless court, where white and free
The clouds sailed northward through the blue of spring.
"Yet I forget—what meant that blustering
Cretan this morn? The lots? The tears and cries?"
But Aegeus cowered from those grey questioning eyes,
With hidden face, and groaned "My son, my son,
You ask my second fault, the fouler one,
That makes men hate me. When Medea fled
Hither, still beautiful—and I, unwed—
I pitied her—was she not true to me,
Till now you crossed her last child's destiny?

Then to the Games of Athens came as guest
Androgeos, son of Minos. Mightiest
Among us all the stranger proved that day
At leaping, wrestling, running—bore away
Prize upon prize, cauldron and ox and slave,
Till men cursed deep to see him so outbrave
Our bravest; muttering he played not straight.
I know not. But I know the greedy hate,
Already, of the sons of Pallas burned
To filch my sceptre from me—quick they turned
To whisper with this Cretan—'Let the King
His father thrust me out, and they would bring
Athens beneath his footstool, be his men.'
It was then Medea brought me ruin, then
That I listened and was lost." Hoarse, husky came
The old King's voice; and shamed to see his shame
The young man bowed his face. "I stooped to kill
By stealth; to murder. Three youths, chafing still
For their defeat, waylaid him secretly,
The Cretan, on the road to Oenoe—
Under Cithaeron, where the tree-hung track
Gropes up the glen towards Thebes. He came not back.
Fool that I was! Would God I had defied
Traitors at home and foes abroad, and died
In open fight on some red battlefield!
The dead was found. Tongues talked. I stood revealed.

36

In the market-place of Athens on its bier
That naked body slept with one dark smear
Of blood across its beauty. In the bay,
From Phalerum to Munychia, soon there lay
The fleet of Minos; and upon my throne
I sat amid my people's hate, alone,
Helpless. I bowed my head. The Lord of Crete
Stood on the Hill of Athens. At his feet
I begged his mercy on this conquered land.
Like those gaunt shapes of granite in the sand
Of Nile, he watched me with his stony eyes,
And pitiless face, and heart that heard no cries.
Blood for his blood, life for the life we slew
He made us pay, and each nine years anew—
Yes, seven youths for the youth that there lay dead,
Seven maids for the bride his son would never wed.
Nine years ago was this: nine years are run—
Now do you understand at last, my son?
The Black Ship comes again; but they return
Never. And how they perish none can learn.
Dark is that realm of Cnossus: what things dwell
Behind its golden glory, none dares tell,
For its Lord holds the keys of Heaven, and treads
	the steps of Hell.
But in some winding cavern of the King
There lurks, they say, a horror—a nameless thing,

Man-like, and yet no man"—(he held his breath)
"Whose face—yet it has no face—to meet is death.
And those that go—" But shouting to his feet
Leapt Theseus—"Then that shape is mine to meet.
Where is this Cretan?" But Aegeus screamed "Ah no!
Not you, not you! I cannot let you go.
All else is gone—I cannot die alone,
For Minos' son I cannot give my own.
Do you hate me—stained with murder? Take my
     place—
Be king in Athens! I will beg for grace
From Minos—let him slay me if he will.
What can it matter? What am I to kill,
Now Athens has a king and I a son?—
Or dreamed I had. But now what I have done,
Has lost his love. Let me go meet my end,
Seeing I have left no wife, no son, no friend.
Death is not hard, for one who once has seen
The futile folly all his life has been."
The young man turned away. But Aegeus took
Those strong brown wrists between white hands
     that shook—
"Think, Theseus. You are bitter. You have learned
To scorn the very things that once you yearned
So much to find. Yet youth is sweet to live,
My son; and yours is no more yours to give.

Remember Athens. Theseus, for a king
His life is not his own for venturing."
His voice sank to a whisper—"Then one day,
When next the Black Ship darkens Phalerum Bay,
Although from Sidon west to Sicily
Minos is lord, as though the very sea
Feared him, who knows what the years may hold in
    store?—
A day may come that bares the blade of war.
Till then, Theseus, be wise." Low Theseus said
"And will that day bring these back from the dead?"
Silent they stood. Through the hush, in Heaven
    above
The eagles screamed. "My father, for the love
Of me your people will rally round your throne
Against the Pallantids, when I am gone.
Then, if I fall, if they grow too strong to meet—
Why, sovereignty is no ill winding-sheet.
Weep not for me. Think—like a dream I came
One day, and vanished—is life not still the same?"
But Aegeus looked at him with eyes grown full—
"You are mad, my son, yet the more lovable.
How shall I bear it, gazing out to sea
For your ship returning?—Ah, but promise me,
(What use to hope?—and yet!) if you prevail,
On the black galley hoist a snow-white sail."

Long then he wept on the shoulder of his son.
They left the hall. The shadows had begun
To lengthen eastwards from the rough-hewn row
Of Athene's temple-columns. Dark and low
Its entrance, darker all its inward room,
With shapes of white that glimmered through the
      gloom—
The gathered victims. Women sobbed and wept,
Or clung in wild embrace, or mutely crept
Like dazed wild things, or knelt in writhing prayer
Before the Goddess, with her changeless stare,
Rough-hewn in olive-wood. Then whispers passed—
As risen from the dead, white and aghast,
Out to the square where the sweet sun shone hot,
A youth by the lot condemned, now saved by lot,
Staggered half doubting his god-given grace,
While with the doomed there Theseus took his place.
Then a sad trumpet called. Their hour was come.
First down the harbour-track swept, proud and
      dumb,
In a gilt litter on the necks of slaves
The Cretan, glad at heart to see the waves
Dancing before him, and his task near done.
Then in a mule-car, hiding from the sun
Those tear-blind faces soon would see him rise
No more, the maidens; then the youths, their eyes

Strained hard before them, sorrowful yet proud,
While round them all the seething street grew loud
With lamentation; last, shamed and dismayed,
While their heedless horses tossed their necks and
    neighed,
Rode the royal guard. Through the rumbling gate
    they went,
Past Victory's barren shrine, down the descent
'Twixt the Nymphs' Hill and the Muses', o'er the
    stream
Ilissus, towards the western waters' gleam
By far Phalerum. Slowly across the plain
They dwindled, and the soft dusk sank again
In silence. Not the bravest dared look back
At the walls of home behind them, crowded black
With watching shapes, where severed from the rest,
With dim eyes gazing towards the sunset west,
Stood the old King.
              So all that night they slept,
Guarded, in fishers' huts or, sleepless, wept.
Behind Cyllene's snows the moon near full,
Gaunt in the glare of dawn as some pale skull,
Sank tombed among the mountains. On the shore
The seamen rose and with a grinding roar
Heaved their ship down the shingle; then on board
The captives huddled, watched with spear and sword

41

By grinning negroes of the Cretan King.
They raised the mast. The sail puffed bellying
Before the breeze of dawn. As fresh and keen
Off high Parnes it blew as it had been
The wind of the first dayspring of the world,
While from the prow gurgled and crunched and curled
The dark-blue ripples. The mountains watched them go:
Silent the circle of those heads of snow
In conclave ringed the sea. Now Sunium,
Last cape of Athens, towered up dark and dumb
Before them, and to westward tall Troezene;
Behind them, like some sea-beast, black, obscene,
Wallowed the long war-galley that from Crete
Had brought the ambassador. But clear and sweet
Amid their grief a voice rose suddenly,
A girl's voice, singing low, then towering free,
Until her fellows half forgot their pain,
Startling the sea-mews with their loud refrain—
    "Farewell, dear land of Athens, set
      Between the hillside and the sea,
   Town of the crown of violet,
      Long may thy Goddess smile on thee.
        Farewell, dear land where I shall stand
          No more. In sweet springs yet to come
        Remember me who shall not see
          Their sunlight strike on Sunium.

Farewell Parnes, Pentelicus,
  Meadows I wandered, woods I knew.
You whispered not the end was thus,
  My flower should fade before it grew.
    Farewell, dear land where I shall stand
      No more. In sweet springs yet to come
    Remember me who shall not see
      Their sunlight strike on Sunium.

I dreamed the hills that gave me birth
  Should take my ashes to their breast:
Our graves are dug in other earth,
  With other dust our dust shall rest.
    Farewell, dear land where I shall stand
      No more. In sweet springs yet to come
    Remember me who shall not see
      Their sunlight strike on Sunium.

Bitter is death in banishment!
  And yet, O Fate, I thank thee still,
If brief my days, my days were spent
  Under Athene's white-walled hill.
    Farewell, dear land where I shall stand
      No more. In sweet springs yet to come
    Remember me who shall not see
      Their sunlight strike on Sunium.

I never craved old age, its care,
    Its falling locks, its failing breath:
One thing alone is hard to bear—
    I knew not Love, ere I knew Death.
        Farewell, dear land where I shall stand
            No more. In sweet springs yet to come
        Remember me who shall not see
            Their sunlight strike on Sunium."

So they watched far across the widening seas,
While the sun climbed and freshlier blew the breeze,
Athens fall dim behind, bright rise the Cyclades.

II

"O tu, che vieni al doloroso ospizio,"
   disse Minos.

                              Dante.

II

ALL day they sailed to southward; till their mast
Flung its black sail's black shadow, gaunt and vast,
Far out across the foam, and sunset's glow
Fretted with jags of flame the line of snow
That walled the western wave—the peaks that stand
To guard Eurotas and the Hollow Land
Of Lacedaemon. Then the north wind fell:
With a grind of oars across the oily swell
The rowers laboured—no hope now to reach
Ere night the warm springs and the welcome beach
Of rock-girt Melos. Towards an isle at hand,
Little and lone, they steered and up its sand
Shouldered their dripping keels. Along the shore
Four twinkling fires, as dusk to darkness wore,
Gleamed out to meet the gathering stars. By one
Lay softly in his pied pavilion
The Cretan. By two others roared and ate
The mariners. Dumb and disconsolate
Beside the last the captives listlessly
Watched the smoke billow and the bright sparks flee
Into the homeless hollows of the night,
Their food forgot; till Theseus, with the light

47

Flashing wild crimson on flushed face and hair,
Cried through their silence—"Idlest is Despair
Of all the Immortals—weak, without wit or will,
Gnawing her own flesh, yet faint and starving still.
Up, eat and drink! For even Niobe
Took food at last, though she had lived to see
Twelve sons and daughters slain the selfsame day;
Took food at last, though now she stands, men say,
On Sipylus, high up its cloudy crest,
Her eyes a fountain, and a stone her breast."
Then one by one unwillingly they set
Strips of red goat's-flesh on the spits, and let
The flame's red tongue lick round them, and broke
        bread,
And from the goat-skins watched the wine gush red;
Till lips were loosed a little, and smiles began
Faintly to flicker on faces worn and wan,
And breasts that a slowly tightening band had
        seemed
To stifle, breathed again—surely they dreamed?—
A dream, not real, that death beyond the lip
Of the dark sea to southward? From their ship
Then Theseus called the master, to a place
Beside them; like a cormorant's that keen face,
With its hooked nose, those eyes that near and far
Knew every reef from Troy to Malea;

To a tapering point his beard fell, bleached and grey
With brine, and on his cheek the stinging spray
Had tanned a thousand wrinkles. Grim he gazed
On those doomed faces where the firelight blazed;
But Theseus poured him wine, and in his ear
Whispered "Now talk! Make them forget their fear,
To-night's foreboding and to-morrow's woe,
With tales of far away and long ago."
So, while his long beard wagged, the old man told
How, past King Atlas' apple-garth of gold,
Beyond the storm-swept Cassiterides,
There sleeps a leaden waste of slimy seas,
Dead seas without leap of fish or dance of foam,
Where rot lost ships, long, long forgot at home,
Like flies held fast in honey; while on high
Above that sluggish sea the sluggish sky
Wheels through a whole six months upon its way
The sleepless, lifeless Hyperborean day;
And how the tears that once the Sun-god shed,
Banished to that bleak world, still overspread
Its ice-ribbed beaches, and men seek them there,
Grown hard and yellow, for white necks to wear
Far off in golden Cnossus. Then he told
How, south of Atlas, blazing rivers rolled
Down to a hissing sea; and on its shore
Wild hairy men leapt from the trees and tore

The stranger piecemeal—then a shudder ran
Through those white faces, and a girl began
To sob aloud. As one that wakes with day
And, drowsy still, yet feels in dim dismay
The shadow of some hawk-like hovering pain
That rent him yesterday, and now again
Hangs overhead; so wretchedly they woke
To the thought of their own doom. The waves that broke
So softly through the silence, and the sough
Of the wind's whisper betwixt leaf and bough
Of the old oak-tree by the waterside,
The waning moon's quiet radiance, dim-descried
Amidst her fleece of silver—could there be
Behind such loveliness such cruelty!
The old man's tongue droned on, unheeded now,
From land to land; till with a scowling brow
Euthycles of Paeania, passionate
Beyond the rest, burst out "What serves this prate
Of nursery tales? We are not babes in bed
To be coaxed and dandled to forget the dread
Our mouths are dry with. Speak!—what waits us there,
In Crete? What death, what horror must we bear
That none dares tell us? You at least must know—
With you those others sailed, nine years ago."
A tumbling wave boomed hollow, far away
An owl wailed through the woodland; fierce and gay

The drunken seamen's laughter round their fires
Rang down the wind. "In vain the heart desires"
Said old Euaemon "to know the coming thing
That Zeus keeps hid. Hark how they shout and sing,
My mariners, while ye sit here downcast:
And yet who knows?—before a day is past,
They may be hurled like sea-wrack, helplessly,
High up some screaming beach, and you go free;
If Fate so will. For by the All-Father's throne
Two Fates stand always: one, not all unknown—
A little way wisdom has power to scan
The web of her tangled weaving, shape her plan;
But, for that other, no man knows her mind,
No God can alter it—black-hooded, blind,
When she raises her dark hand, the conqueror falls
While the proud trumpet of his conquest calls,
The ship sinks in mid-harbour, and the bride
Dies on her bride-night by her bridegroom's side.
I had a wife. The Tyrrhene rovers came—
'Tis ten years now—and Rhamnus rose in flame.
I found my home grey ashes: now, forlorn,
In some strange land they grind a master's corn,
Those hands I loved. Two sons I had—afar
Under the angry crags of Malea
Their bones bleach now. Yet still I eat my bread,
Still love the sun—no sun shines on the dead.

I have learnt the world—take thought, where
      thought avails,
Then think no more. The wind may swell my sails
To-morrow, or may split them—as it will!
To-night I take my ease, and eat my fill.
Ask me no more to know this hidden thing.
None knows. None knows. And knowledge could
      not bring
Counsel nor comfort. Wiser is the beast
That fears no future, mourns not what has ceased,
But, belly-filled, is happy." "No!—tell all!"
Shouted another. "Nothing can befall
So dreadful as our dreams of what may be.
Speak, speak—you have heard some rumour—"Silently,
With knitted brows the old man watched them there,
As one that has found the world too harsh to spare
Compassion easily; yet pities still
With quiet, brooding eyes its weight of ill:
So some lone thorn-tree on a barren moor,
Gnarled and wind-writhen, struggling to endure
Its bitter sky, yet yields a moment's rest
To wayworn men, and to the wren its nest.
"There lies a cave" he said "high up the peak
Of Iuktas. There no goat-herd dares to seek
Goats that have strayed; no mountain-fox, men say,
Makes there his lair; there broods no bird of prey.

Only the wind whistles its weary song
About that hidden Hell-mouth all year long.
Ice-fanged in winter, bleached with summer sun,
So it lies lonely, till nine years have run
And in the Bull the Sun renews his might,
While equal flow the tides of day and night;
Then Minos, Lord of Cnossus, King of Crete,
Climbs that curst crag, and passes in, to meet—
No man knows what. In Cnossus I have heard,
Sometimes, and through the Isles, a whispered
      word,
No more—that deep within that cavern's womb
Some strange shape moves to meet him through the
      gloom,
A shape with horns. Some say it is our God—
Europa's horned lover, He whose nod
Makes all Olympus shudder like a steer
The gad-fly stings—and there in Minos' ear
Zeus breathes what laws His people shall obey
That Heaven may guard their greatness. Others say
It is our Lord the Sun, who in that cave
Stores his hid strength, that every year bids wave
Like a sea the corn of Cnossus, and makes glow
Purple her vines, her oil-vats overflow.
Yet in dim by-streets, taverns where the sun
Peers not, my ears heard darker rumours run.

'Not God, but beast,' they muttered, 'a monstrous
    thing,
Abhorred—that in the palace of the King
One shrieking midnight years ago was born,
The shame of Crete, a hissing and a scorn
To all that hate her—for a queen's own womb,
Under God's curse, brought forth that shape of
    doom.'
They say lost wanderers nighted on the hills
Have heard far off a bellowing that fills
The lonely glens of Iuktas. God or beast?—
Or both, for aught I know? I know at least
I was bound for Lycia once. The north wind swept
Our ship three days to southward, till we crept
Hugging the Cretan coast. There, in the dead
Of night, on the hill of Cnossus flickered red
What looked far off a pillar; then, a man,
Gigantic, horned, with thighs that seemed to span
The whole dark hill-top, framed of red-hot brass—
The midnight sea glared back like molten glass,
While off the land a mystic music came
Of shawms and cymbals round those feet of flame.
Then our spirits sickened in us—for we guessed
That shape of fire against his burning breast
Was gripping, in no lover's fond embrace,
Some quick and quivering flesh, some shrieking face,

As in the cursed rites of them that dwell
In Canaan. There is no more to tell—
'Tis that Bull-god himself that lurks, maybe,
High on the mountain of the mystery.
I only know, of all the flower-bound train
That climbs with Minos from the Cnossian plain,
Not one—" But, cursing, Theseus clapped his hand
Across the old man's mouth: for white, unmanned
They stared into the firelight. But aloud
A girl's voice cried, among those faces cowed,
"No, he is right. Far best to know the worst—
And I do know it. In that land accurst
Let wait what will for us—*we* need not wait.
The narrowest dungeon has its hidden gate—
The Gate of Death! And here there hangs a key
Can pick all locks 'twixt us and liberty."
Up from the hollow of her breasts she drew
A long thin blade. All down its edge of blue
The firelight flickered, till it seemed aflame,
While charging up its length a lioness came,
Wrought in bright gold; from her flank the blood ran red,
But before that dying charge the huntsmen fled,
Save one that waited, calm, with spear in rest.
"This farewell gift," she said, with heaving breast,
"This, out of all his wealth, my father gave—
A Cretan dagger for the Cretan's slave—

Whispering 'Death, dear child, comes kindest to
      the brave.'"
Down her white neck, to lie beside her heart
She let it slide. But with a sudden start
Courage came back to all her fellows there—
Their straightening shoulders shook aside despair,
Their brightening eyes outfaced it—life seemed grown
Rich with new fellowship, too rich to moan
Its own poor loss; half-shamed, and half with pride,
They saw the doom they shrank before, defied
By one girl's heart. But Theseus with his eyes
Fastened upon her mused in still surprise
How she had won them where he strove in vain,
Bidding them, not forget, but face their pain.
A gust whirled in his face a wreath of smoke—
Its pleasant-smarting smell of wood awoke
A sleeping memory—he saw again
The black fir-forest where his strength had slain
The Pinetree-bender; and that woodland thing
Whose slim brown arms so sweetly learnt to cling
Round him, that night, by such a fire as this.
Where were they now those eyes so soft to kiss?
"I turned away," he thought "I left it all
For love of Athens, for the silent call
Deep in my heart, that bade me seek my sire.
Alas, I followed only a wandering fire,

A fool's bright fancy. And now to crown my quest
I have found Death Himself. Ah, had I guessed!"—
Yet, as he watched her in the firelight's gleam,
He dreamed that here at last was more than dream;
Those lips too frank to lie, that eager face
No cares would coarsen, and no years debase
In its proud loyalty—they were not fair
As some, no woodland creature's grace lay there;
And yet there lived in those dark steadfast eyes
A lovelier thing than beauty, to the wise.
She half turned towards him with a swift shy look,
Feeling his silence—in his hand he took
Her slim wrist, whispering beneath his breath
"Aegle!—'I knew not Love ere I knew Death'—
This morn you sang it—ah, to-night no more!"
And all at once it seemed that, where before
Great wings of Death had shadowed all the world,
Grey-feathered with the thousand cloud-wisps curled
High up the moon-lit heavens, now instead
Across the night the wings of Eros spread.
The wind had fallen; glittering round the Pole
Arcturus swung; and slowly silence stole
Across the fading embers, whose red glow
Like a dying dragon's eye, as gusts breathed low,
Opened and shut and seemed to watch in fear
The feather-footed darkness creeping near.

Then side by side in silence youth and maid
Like phantoms vanished in its sheltering shade,
Unchallenged and unchecked—so small the isle
That held them prisoned. For this little while
Even the swarthy guard, with pitying eye,
Let them pass, lovers now, so soon to die.
 But with the dawn a wind rose from the south,
Lashing before it, with foam-flecked mane and mouth,
The sea's white horses, and across the sky
Herding its white cloud-fleeces endlessly,
Shaking the birds' young nests, and fluttering
The grey sea-grasses with the shout of spring.
Three days it blew, and held them wind-bound there
'Twixt life and death; but now the old despair
Had fallen from them. To distract their thought
Rough seamen in their simple pity brought
Strange shells and bright-finned fishes; when
  night fell,
Round their camp-fire the negro-chief would tell
With his white-gleaming smile, of his own land
Where the serpent Nile writhed through the
  scorching sand
Past pale Syene; of the tribes that hide
In Libya's darkness—how the Psylli died
Warring against the South Wind in the waste;
How the Garamantes in their chariots chased

58

The Troglodytes, matchless of men for speed,
Dwarf, gibbering things that squeak like bats, and
    feed
On serpents; how the Atarantes bear
No names, and curse the Sun whose coppery glare
Turns all their land to flame. But in his tent
Brooding all day in moody discontent,
The Cretan lord lay eyeing that waste of foam,
Cursing the wind that held him still from home;
While those doomed souls forgot the flying feet
Of the brief hours, plucking the meadow-sweet
Along the marshy edges of the bay—
Flowers that could look for longer life than they.
    But the third eve brought change; to south and west
The sky grew ribbed with grey; upon the breast
Of Theseus, underneath the lonely shade
Of a sea-withered cypress, Aegle laid
Her head and watched the clouds form silently,
While the wind's failing breath across the sea
Piped through the boughs its listless low lament.
But no care touched the eager face that bent
Fondly above her. Kissing each finger-tip
Between his words, he let his fancy slip
Laughing into the future—with sail of white their ship
Rounded Phalerum; up the shouting street,
With flowers in showers beneath their horses' feet,

Their chariot climbed—past Victory's rose-hung shrine
To the grey palace of Erechtheus' line,
Where the old Aegeus stood to clasp his son,
His guilt forgotten and the past undone—
"And but for you, dear heart, this had not been.
Yours, love, the vision—in your eyes 'twas seen.
So shall Aegeus find a daughter, and Athens find a queen."
Sadly she smiled and, smiling, shook her head,
As a mother at her child. "Ah, love," she said
"God grant it so!" Down-glancing he descried
Deep in her eyes black hopelessness, and cried
"O foolish heart, that gave me faith again
And yet itself despairs! All seemed so vain
That dusk we landed on this lonely shore—
I could have wept, so bitter and so sore
My heart to find the world such mockery,
Till, love, the love of you gave back to me
Something to live for, die for—not a name,
Like Athens, or like Aegeus—not, like fame,
A phantom faint and fickle as the breath
That breeds it; but one heart, through life and death,
To know and trust and love beyond my own.
Ah, steep the road to feet that climb alone!
I have learnt—against the world one is too few,
A host too many; none so strong as two.
I thought I sought for Athens—O love, I looked for you."

Then, seeing her smile once more, he caught her wrist
Laughing, and bent above her eyes, and kissed
Their searching sadness blind—"Dear, traitor eyes,
You doubt. But I—I know. Whether it be
My own heart hears the step of Victory
Far off, as of old my hounds in high Troezene
Would scent with a sudden quiver, though unseen,
The wild deer's track far up the misty glen;
Or whether some voice within me, not of men,
Has whispered 'Hope!'—O love, be not afraid.
For surely she to whom my mother prayed,
She that loved Athens once—and loves it still—
Grey-eyed Athene, will not see this ill
Endure for ever? Surely the Gods are just,
Who have planted deep within our human dust
This deathless cry for justice?" In the west,
Like red-hot iron, the sun sank towards his rest;
The cold grey clouds above, grey waves below,
Crimsoned like blood before that furnace-glow.
But Aegle sighed "Ah, justice? Who can say?
What had they done, whom the Black Ship bore
        away
Nine years ago before us, youth and maid?
Yet who knows now where their thin dust is laid?
What had my father and my mother done,
That one should die, one live to loathe the sun?

Lovely as dawn she was, and sweet as spring,
Yet Artemis whom wives in child-bearing
Call to their help, helped *her* not—with no flame
Of life's torch newly lit that night She came,
But with her deadly arrows. White and dead
Mother and child, they lay on that still bed.
Lone in Aphidna then my father dwelt,
To the Gods all honour, justice to men he dealt;
But the honour that he gave, the Gods forgot,
The justice that he did, he found it not.
Of all that loved him, I alone was left
To cheer his age. The lots were drawn. Bereft
Now of me too, he sits beside his fire
Brooding how life leaves us but one desire
At last, the one desire it thwarts not—Death.
Ah love, forget to-morrow. Waste not breath
To say you will love me always—can you know?
Yet bless you, that you dream it, wish it, so!
Say that you love me now, love me to-day,
For that not Zeus Himself can take away—
Sooner the Gods shall make an end of me,
O love, my love, than of that memory.
But well I know, though by Athene's will
You slay that Horror, and we see the hill,
Once more, of Athens, yet in Heaven there sits
Another Goddess, whose light favour flits

62

From face to face, as once across the foam
From wave to wave her white feet bore her home
To Cyprus—She can witch your heart away
(Deep lie the earth above me ere that day!)
To a fairer face than mine; for in your eyes,
Only in yours, O love, my beauty lies."
"No, in your own," he cried "where shines so clear
Your own true heart, so brave, so loyal, so dear—
Eyes where the light of the Graces lives for me;
The Cyprian is but one, and they are three!"
His arms were round her—after summer-drouth
As the parched earth drinks the rain, beneath his mouth
Her yearning face lay dumb and blind and still.
But off the twilit deep the wind blew chill
Across the rustling sallows by the sea
Where the reeds shook their tall heads drearily.
Cheek against cheek, beyond Cape Malea
Under the first glint of the evening star
They watched the last light of the sunset smile
On far Cythera, Aphrodite's isle;
Till heaven above, the wrinkled waves beneath
Before the feet of Night grew grey as Death.
    Then through the darkness fell the fine small rain,
Quiet, pitiless; as though no sun again
Could ever pierce that blackness like a pall
That crushed the mountains flat, muffling the fall

Of the faint waves upon the sodden sand,
While rock and bush and tree along the strand
Wept with great drops; heavy, insistent, dull.
So hour by hour, huddled within the hull
Of the Black Ship, they shivered for the morn,
Though Death came with it. Crouched there, wet
    and worn,
Little dreamed Theseus how in after-days,
'Mid all his glory, a mist would dim his gaze
Sometimes, and longing choke him, at the thought
Of that bleak night beneath the rowers' thwart,
With that hand lost in his. At last the day
Thinned night's dark mantle into threadbare grey;
Then with a breath that suddenly tarnished black
The still sea's silver mirror, and flung back
The curtains of the heavens, keen and cold
The North wind rose. Shouting the seamen rolled,
Glad to be gone, their galleys down the steep,
And once again the brazen beaks drank deep,
While the sea-mews screamed around them. Hand
    in hand
Theseus and Aegle watched that little land
Turn blue against the distance, left again
Alone with sun and wave and wind and rain,
Lizard and lark, wild-rose and cypress-tree,
As if no voice had stirred its secrecy;

Thinking how in three days that rock unknown
Had grown their friend, its loneliness their own;
And now for ever in the heart of each
That bleak hill-top would flower, that barren beach.
  So they drove south amid the Cyclades
That right and left across the sunlit seas
Lay basking like great lions, with tawny paws
Of rock that the blue wave washed, and hidden claws
Of reef where gleamed white the foam—beyond the steep
Of Siphnos, and the triple peaks that keep
Watch o'er Amorgos; leaving leftward far
Thera, where wrestle in eternal war
Poseidon and Hephaestus, Sea and Fire.
Its smoke-cloud rose to heaven, spire on spire,
Like a dark-branching cedar, as they came,
While from its surges broke not foam, but flame.
But in the haze to southward, hour by hour,
Grew from the blue, like a white lily-flower,
The snows of Ida: and they whispered "Crete."
The daylight died; but still beneath their feet
Homeward the rollers raced, while they drove on
And grim in heaven across their pathway shone,
Like a giant warder of the Cretan Lord,
Orion, girded with his glittering sword;
Till far lights twinkled and with canvas furled
They waited for the dawn to wake the world,

While in the darkness slowly heaved and fell,
Like a great breast asleep, the silent swell
Of an unknown sea. Then lo! a flush of rose
Far to their right kindled the topmost snows
Of Ida; and before them, with a shroud,
Clinging about its feet, of pale white cloud
A nearer summit towered. Sharp in the air
Of the green dawn its crowning ridge stood bare,
Shaped like a face of stone—a face that lay
As in a slumber that the brightening day
Must break each moment now—and yet too deep
For eternity to wake its cloud-encircled sleep.
Then in the darkness by the dipping prow
To Euaemon Theseus whispered "What strange brow
Of stone gleams high in Heaven?" Beneath his breath
"Iuktas" the old man answered. "There in death
The Cretans say the ancient ashes lie
Of Zeus Himself; and there against the sky
Slumbers His face for ever." Swift in scorn,
The voice of Euthycles through that red dawn
Rang out, "The Cretan liars! All the world
Shall end, and Heaven from its height be hurled,
Ere He that shakes Olympus with His nod,
Dies. For what death dare touch the lips of God?"
But the old man answered with slow-shaken head
"I tell the tale they told me. Zeus lies dead

On Iuktas. Yet He dies not. For the tomb
That hides Him dead is but His new life's womb.
Again the Mother bears the child She bore,
Again Her son grows as He grew of yore,
Hid in the hollow of the pathless hills,
Through the blossom of bright boyhood, till He fills
The world with His full-flushed splendour, and grows old
And fades away. I tell the tale they told.
Who knows? The corn's white beard dies back to earth,
Yet, buried, brings the young green blade to birth."
"And old men likewise" with a bitter smile
Said Euthycles, "turn children. Go beguile
Babes with such tales. No lies can cure life's pain.
We know we die to-morrow, and no dead live again."
But like the folds of some great winding-sheet
That white mist lifted from the mountains' feet
And, whiter yet, in the glimmering dawn grew clear
The harbour-town of Cnossus, tier on tier
Of gleaming stone; as though, if that sleeping God
Rose from the mountain, His feet might have trod
That shining staircase downward to the sea.
    Then as they gazed, from the Cretan war-galley
A trumpet pealed; far up the harbour-side
Faint and more faint its failing echoes died.
Black grew the quays, black grew the roofs with folk,
Windows flew wide, as all the port awoke.

Then with slow-dipping oars the two ships drew
Shoreward, while round them against the cloudless blue
Towered the tall mastheads of the ships of Crete
That held the boundless seas at Minos' feet,
Flat to his will as the web of purple strown
Before the footstool of his kingly throne—
Ships come from Sidon, ships the Atlantic foam
Beyond Tartessus had shouldered rolling home,
Groaning with gold and ivory, ships that Po
And seven-mouthed Nile had mirrored in their flow,
That past Abydus, past the Symplegades
Had braved the gales that scourge the Friendless Seas
From Cimmeria to Colchis. Grim they stood
With their bare masts, as stands some barren wood
A fire has blasted—leafless, lifeless tower
The serried fir-tops, though beneath them flower
Bluebell and crocus round the feet of death;
So those bare masts stood ranged there, while no breath
Came whispered from the watching multitude
That lined the harbour-side, as many-hued
As an April meadow; Death too waited there.
The splash of oars alone shook the still air,
As to the quay they glided. Dumb and dazed
After two nights of watching, Theseus gazed
On that hushed concourse; blurred before his sight,
As in a dream, there shimmered priests in white,

Hands sprinkling holy water, heads low bowed
While high behind them waved above the crowd
Weird symbols and wild shapes of mystery,
Bull's horns and double axes, dove and snake and tree.
Yet stranger still the human shapes around,
Beardless, dark-skinned, with belts that tightly bound
Their snaky middles, sinister to see
As ants with the measure of humanity,
And that deep musing look in every eye
With which men living watch men doomed to die;
As if, within the shadow of Death's wings,
They must glimpse some secret vision of the things
Beyond the grave. But suddenly there jarred
Sharp on the stones the spear-butts of the guard;
Up the staring street they passed; the houses thinned;
The fields were round them. Lightly breathed the wind
Across the young green corn, like the caress
Of an unseen hand on its lithe loveliness.
The lark trilled high above their clanking chains
And, higher yet, big with the glad spring rains,
The white clouds climbed, white as the blossoming trees,
Borne on the shoulders of the shouting breeze
Up the blue wall of Heaven. They looked away,
To the dust beneath their feet: such dust were they—
Long ere those green blades turned to golden ears,
Dust all their memory, dry their kindred's tears.

Like a snake the white road wound. A turn, and lo!
The city of King Minos. Row on row,
Up his far palace-roofs against the sky
Rose marble horns of mystic sanctity;
As though white bulls of more than mortal size
Mounted the hill for some strange sacrifice.
Beneath, the swarming crowds choked black the ways,
Heads craned from every casement. There to gaze
The smith had left his forge, the groom his steed;
In the empty market lay with none to heed
The warm brown loaves, fish with wet scales agleam;
Kine lowed deserted; dumb as in a dream,
With eyes that strained to see the strangers clear,
Yet shifted sideways with a nameless fear,
That multitude bowed as one man before
The cold white priests that up the long street bore
The Banner of the Sacred Knot unfurled,
The Knot that none shall loosen till the world
Itself be loosed in sunder at the last.
So through that hush of death the prisoners passed
Within the palace-gate, and down its stair,
Out of the warm sun and the scented air,
To darkness. Icy as the lifeless lake
Where the parched wanderer plunges home to slake
The heat of August on the barren hills—
Deep in its black embrace the water chills

His shuddering body till he gasps for breath—
So felt that vault with its black damp of death.
Then slow hour followed hour; through one
      small hole,
Like a long lance of light, the sunbeams stole
At noon athwart the darkness; mad with glee
Down it there danced, in witless mockery,
A million motes, till they too paled away
And in the chink, left dusty now and grey,
A single spider sat and waited for his prey.
Outside, a blackbird whistled. Hurrying feet,
Shouting and laughter, far-off, strangely sweet,
Pierced faintly to them through the pitiless stone.
As a sick man dying in the grey dawn, alone,
Hears to his work some drudge go singing clear,
And feels "Ah how unutterably dear—
Past price—only to live!"—so, listening there,
Life's careless echoes choked them with despair.
Dim grew their inch of sky; their prison-door
Gaped for an instant—groping on the floor
Their hands found bread and water. Then one star
Peered in upon their sorrow, faint and far.
Some slept. In the arms of Theseus Aegle lay,
Hardly unhappy, dreaming that no day
Should rob her, now, of him her heart had found,
Nor God's self sunder those whom Death had bound.

The brazen hinges grated—with a groan
The door swung wide—upon the sweating stone
Wet glanced the gleam of torches. Up the stair
Guarded they passed and, blinking in the glare,
Through echoing passages with shapes that leapt
To sudden life as the shimmering torchlight swept
Far down their darkness and the shadows fled
Like ghosts before it; for to meet them came,
Carved on the walls, great bulls with eyes aflame,
Or snub-nosed dolphins plunging through the blue,
Till the following tide of darkness swallowed them
    anew.
Onward they went, through endless winding ways,
Through door on door they passed, through maze
    on maze,
Till on a sudden lo! a hall before,
Dim-lit with tapers. At their backs, a door
Shut thundering. They stood at last, alone,
Before King Minos and the Cretan throne.
High overhead the roof rose into gloom,
Columned with cypress; as within his tomb
Some king long buried, he sat silent there
And in the crown that girt his greying hair
Pale gleamed the sacred lilies of the dead.
As lifeless seemed he as, behind his head,
The two stone griffins carved with beaks that curled,

The sleepless Warders of the Underworld.
Next him his Queen, below his judgment-seat
Sat ranged and still the royal blood of Crete—
Deucalion, Glaucus, pale Xenodice,
Dark Acacallis—she that secretly,
Men say, loved an Immortal in the glen
Beneath Mount Ida, far from feet of men,
And left her babe to perish, sore afraid
Of her stern father, in that woodland glade
Where came no more her lover. Red and wild
Her eyes gleamed yet with weeping for her child;
Not knowing a wood-wolf nursed that wailing thing
To be hereafter warrior and king
And build wide-walled Miletus. By her there,
One golden head amidst their raven hair,
One pale fair face amidst their swarthiness,
Watched the white Ariadne. Tenantless
One place alone was left, one seat unfilled,
At the King's right, for him whose blood was spilled
Nine years ago in Athens. On each hand
Stood the pale priests and dark lords of the land.
Slowly upon each captive's face in turn
The eyes of Minos brooded, as to learn
What hidden thoughts each inmost heart could hold—
Stern without pity, without cruelty cold.
Then in a harsh deep voice "Ye go", he said,

"To-morrow to the nations of the dead.
Your elders sinned; ye suffer; seems it hard?
Fear not: your souls shall find their own reward,
For good or evil. Better to atone,
Dying now, for sins of others than, after, for your own."
Even as he spoke, the oldest priest of all,
White-haired, white-stoled, passed noiseless down
　　　the hall,
And with a knife of gold from each doomed head
Severed a single lock, and with it fed
The small red worm of incense-breathing flame,
That burnt before Her feet whom none dares name—
The Mother, carved there with Her Triple Crown;
From whose bare ivory arms two snakes hung down
Wreathing Her wrists, and on Her diadem
A dove sat perched, and beneath Her long robe's hem
Lay shells awhisper of the far-off sea,
Signs of Her godhead's mystic Trinity—
For mistress She of sea and earth and air.
Crackling the flame devoured each lock of hair,
Then died to dust. But Theseus thrust aside
The old priest's palsied hand and with one stride
Stood forth before the throne and stretched an arm
Towards Minos and with ringing voice, yet calm,
"O King," he cried, "they say from East to West
Of kings that deal men justice, one deals best—

74

The Lord of Cnossus! Spoke they truth or lie
Of one that dooms men innocent to die?"
Slowly the voice made answer from the throne
"For blood your fathers shed, their sons atone.
Dream not you die for nothing. In your place
Others must perish though I gave you grace.
Nine years are gone: the Dweller in the Cave
Craves sacrifice. In vain He must not crave,
Lest Heaven's Queen grow angry, and Her hand
Fall like a sword across the Cretan land."
But Theseus answered "Are the gods less just
Than men they made love justice? Can they lust
To drink of women's blood?" Still as a stone
That stands on some stormy headland, all alone,
God of a vanished nation, heeding not
The winds that wail about its face forgot,
Sat Minos. Only from those dark eyes sped
One glance to the waiting guard, and that dark head
Nodded towards the doorway. Then a cry
Burst from the lips of Aegle—"Let us die,
But he—O King, he is not what you dream."
Then Theseus caught her wrist. But with a scream
She broke away—"There stands the son, O King,
Of Aegeus, Lord of Athens. Will you bring
The anger of our Gods upon your land?
For They are with him—by that smooth young hand

75

Fell Periphetes of the Iron Mace
In Epidaurus, at the narrow place
High up the Spider Mountains, where he drew
His web of death; and Sinnis, he that slew
Men 'twixt two pine-trees, 'twixt two pine-trees died;
And Sciron at the Isthmus; and beside
The hill of Crommyon its ravening boar;
And Kerkyon of Eleusis on the shore
Where he had crushed the ribs of other men;
And high up Mount Aegaleus in his den
Procrustes perished, stretched upon the bed
Where he had hacked or racked his own guests dead.
For this is Theseus, whom long since the Queen
Aethra brought forth in mountain-walled Troezene,
Daughter of Pittheus and that house whose fame
Bears through all lands the proud Achaean name—
Eurystheus' cousin, whose high sovranty
Has made Mycenae feared through every sea,
Even the Cretan—" As she named the name
Of Achaea and Mycenae, swift there came
Across those lords of Crete a deeper hush;
Like his that hears within the trembling bush
The lion's low growl. But with quick-heaving breast
Still Aegle spoke—"Ah think, O kingliest,
Shall the world whisper 'Wrong has paid for wrong.
Men called King Minos just—he was but strong'?

Be just indeed, forgive, forget his birth—
Has not he too done justice on the earth?
Let him go back, lest Athens lack a king—
Take us, take us!" But with hands tightening
King Minos gripped the Sphinxes of his throne.
"The Fates are just" he cried. "Unsought, unknown,
The murderer's son stands at the judgment seat
Of the father of the murdered. So we meet,
So blood for blood and son for son is paid."
Then choking back his hate—"All shall be weighed
In the cold scales of justice. Son for son,
The debt stands cancelled, and the guilt undone.
And you—you are young, and innocent, and brave;
Your life I cannot give. Yet in the grave
Sleep well—safe stands henceforward the land you
      came to save."
—Dead-still the hall. Only Pasiphae,
With heavy-lidded eyes fixed dreamily
On the fair face of Theseus, bent aside
And whispered to her lord—her whisper died,
Her face went white, before the cold surmise,
The scorching scorn deep in her husband's eyes.
Then Aegle hid her face. But with a spring
From a guard's hand Theseus wrenched quivering
The spear, and flung him reeling back, and pressed
That glittering death against the golden breast

Of Minos, crying "Stir but a step—he dies!
And you, King Minos, you that are so wise
A judge, judge now—will you perish on your throne,
As you *shall* perish, helpless and alone;
Or swear by Heaven's Queen—there where she
    stands
Before us, with Hell's serpents in her hands—
To let us sail, none hindering, home to Greece,
And leave henceforth the Attic land in peace?"
But slowly Minos spoke: "Do what you will.
Your lives are mine no more, to spare or kill:
Death's Queen has claimed them. With each lock
    that curled
Flaming upon Her altar, to the world
Of Death a soul was sealed and dedicate.
Me you may kill: you cannot kill your fate.
Deucalion, hark! If I die here, my son,
See that the service of the Gods is done;
With justice, not with vengeance." Face to face
They stood confronted in that silent space,
Like two shapes hewn in stone; till Theseus paled
Before that changeless face that never quailed
Beneath his lifted spear; while all around
The eyes of priest and lord, without a sound,
Watched him like waiting wolves. Should he give in,
Throw down his arms, since nought was left to win?

Or thrust hard home and send a king before
To the House of Hades, his ambassador?
Then best it seemed to fall in open fight—
Like a snake's tongue flickered against the light
His back-drawn spear. But swift as thought, between
Her father and the spearhead's deadly sheen
Sprang Ariadne, and caught fast with bare
White hands the plunging point, as in mid-air
The thrust of Theseus faltered. From behind
Then leapt the dark Deucalion and twined
Long arms about him, deadly-deft as when
On some high day of festival the men
Of Cnossus filled their amphitheatre's ring
To watch their great bulls dance before the King,
Till the young Princes of the Cretan land
Grappling those horns of doom with fearless hand
Should wrench their necks in sunder. On the ground
Crashed Theseus headlong, wrestling, writhing round
The Cretan's supple serpent limbs in vain.
A dozen arms had gripped him. With a chain
Fast round his wrists, hard-panting, on his feet
They set him. Then, before the judgment-seat,
For the last time, as through the opened door
The spearmen goaded them, he turned once more
And cried "Minos, farewell! Men call you wise,
Because they fear your might, your mysteries,

O King and Priest, Keeper of Heaven and Hell;
We are young in Hellas, too young yet to spell
Your wisdom—yours the glory and the power!
Yet we are free, we have not learnt to cower
Before kings' sceptres and priests' mummeries—
Our gods ask not bowed heads nor cringing knees!
Let all Crete fawn before you. Poor are we,
But all your gold buys not our liberty,
Nor all your slaves can tame us, though yours the
    tameless sea.
Are you so proud your Cnossus needs no wall?—
The prouder, the sooner comes your hour to fall;
Until this palace crumbles, lost, alone,
And the lizard treads, and the wild fig splits, its stone
And the greybeard thistle nods in purple on your
    throne."
And then, to Ariadne, with a smile—
"Brave heart, fair head, true eyes that know no guile,
What bred you with these wolves? May God give you,
One day, a lover as brave and fair and true!"
They dragged him out. She stood beside her sire
With eyes that stared at the red altar-fire,
Ears that scarce heard his footsteps die away,
So loud the headlong pulses' hammering play
Within her brain. She stooped and whispered low
To her father's changeless face, "Ah let him go,

Spare him, my father—he is so young to die.
Dearly I loved—you know it well as I—
Androgeos, of all my brothers best—
He cared for me when I was loneliest.
Yet now—" But, rising, Minos shook his head,
Laying his cold hand upon her hand that bled
Cut by the spear—"You ask what cannot be."
She quailed before his look; yet mutinously
Quivered her lip—then low beneath her breath
"Fool!" whispered Acacallis "plead with Death,
Not with our father—Death may heed your call."
Pasiphae smiled darkly. Down the hall
The torches danced and died. Aloof, alone,
In the red light before the empty throne,
The Queen of Heaven smiled, with changeless lips
    of stone.

III

τὼ δ' ἄνεῳ καὶ ἄναυδοι ἐφέστασαν ἀλλήλοισιν,
ἢ δρυσίν, ἢ μακρῇσιν ἐελδόμενοι ἐλάτῃσιν,
αἵτε παρᾶσσον ἔκηλοι ἐν οὔρεσιν ἐρρίζωνται,
νηνεμίῃ· μετὰ δ' αὖτις ὑπὸ ῥιπῆς ἀνέμοιο
κινύμεναι ὁμάδησαν ἀπείριτον· ὧς ἄρα τώγε
μέλλον ἅλις φθέγξασθαι ὑπὸ πνοιῇσιν Ἔρωτος.

Apollonius Rhodius.

Speechless and still they stood there, face to face,
Like two tall oaks or firs, that side by side
Stand rooted and at peace, high up the hills,
When winds are hush'd; till a gust suddenly
Wakes in them infinite voices—so they two
Were to find voice, before the winds of Love.

83   6-2

III

But Ariadne tossed upon her bed
Sleepless. Like some white phantom of the dead
Back to her vision rose the stranger's face,
Passionate, pleading, in its pale young grace—
She sobbed. Then thought "Why should he move
    me so?—
Why more than those poor helpless souls that go
With him to death? Why more than she that cried
His name aloud—brave heart, that would have died
To save her prince! And yet—" She sank to sleep
And, slumbering, dreamed that she had ceased to
    weep,
For once again the stranger seemed to stand
By Minos' throne—but now to claim her hand
As his own Queen in Athens. Angrily
Her father frowned. But with a bitter cry
She sprang between—"Whom better will you find,
My father?—some scented Cretan with a mind
Set but on painted women and baited bulls
And slaying of men to feast the eyes of fools!"
And then she dreamed once more the stranger came
Dragging a great bull towards that altar-flame.

He looked at her—with her own hand she gave
A knife, and shuddering watched the red blood lave
Its snowy chest—till all at once her name
Seemed hooted loud with hissing shouts of shame
By all the throats of Cnossus. So she dreamed
And crying woke—it was an owl that screamed.
She flung the casement wide and stood there, pale,
Crowned with the starlight, plucking at the veil
That clouded her bright hair, with trembling hands.
Dim through the darkness stretched the indifferent lands
Of Cnossus far beneath her, and on high
Up its black shoulder Iuktas heaved the sky;
While through the midnight hush she seemed to hear,
Borne on the warm night-wind, far off yet clear,
The muffled howl of Death from that lone cave.
She shuddered. Death in war, a sunlit grave—
They were not hard. But that!—The south wind's breath
Smoothing her cheek, playing with her curls, made death
Seem but a dream no young heart need believe.
She turned away—"What use? Why should I grieve?
He is but one of many—soon or late,
Grey-haired or golden, down the road of fate
He must have gone. What of it? Let him go.
Is life so sweet! How sweet, ah God, I know,
That loathe it." Yet his face before her rose—
Might not life still be sweet with eyes like those

Gazing in hers, with no spear thrust between—
Eyes unforgot, though but one moment seen?
Quietly she wept. But from the gloom behind
A gay voice said "What do you look to find
By the window, Ariadne? In the skies
Reading your fortune? Or was it in the eyes
Of the young Greek? O sister!" From her bed
Laughing the little Phaedra raised her head,
Black-curled on its white pillow. "I saw all,
Hidden behind a curtain by the wall.
O Ariadne, will they kill him now?"
Then Ariadne answered, with her brow
Pressed hard against her hand, "Yes, he will die.
Ah God, that it could be, not he, but I!
Hush, sleep, my little sister! What know you
Of death? Forget! For if our father knew
What thoughts rise in my heart—" But Phaedra
    smiled—
"You think me always nothing but a child!
But I know well what death is. And I know
Why you cry, Ariadne. Listen, though.
There is one man could save him." At the
    word
The elder ceased her sobbing—nothing stirred
For a moment, save the curtain's rustling hem
In the night-wind, and one tall waving stem

Of hyacinth against the window-bars.
"Go to the old man that has named the stars,
That gave our father's ships new wings, and bade
Rivers flow uphill to our doors, and made
Our statues walk. For he knows everything,
And when I am tired of play, sometimes I bring
My dolls and sit there watching how he blows
His furnace angry-red, till hard bronze flows
As soft as milk. He loves you—Oh I know—
Best of us all, though he is grey and old,
(I asked him once); for you have hair of gold
Like the women of Achaea. Quick, now!—run!
For fear the handsome stranger be undone.
O Ariadne, though I laugh, I swear
I would he were not. One as tall and fair
May Our Lady send me when I come to wed!"
Her sister smiled; then from behind her bed
With set lips took the lamp and round her face
Drew a dark cloak and with a thief's soft pace
Slipped from the chamber. All along the walls
The painted monsters woke as her footfalls
Sped by them. Through the garden, up the street,
Under the stars she climbed with stumbling feet.
Dogs bayed, as though the pale Queen of the
    Dead
Were passing. Houses ceased. Onward she sped

Towards one low lonely roof where still a light
From one small window winked upon the night.
She glanced within. An old man, bald and grey,
Under a lamp pored on a gull that lay
With white wings wide outspread upon his knee.
She tapped: to the door he limped, peering to see
What wanderer woke the night—without a word
He led her in, and bade her sit, and stirred
The sleepy embers. Then with quick-drawn breath
"I come" she said "to ask what may mean death,
For either of us. Have you heard what chanced
To-night in Minos' hall?" Nodding he glanced
At her fair firelit face, with keen brown eyes,
Smiling a little to see the deep flush rise
From neck to forehead as she strove to speak:
"He must not die. Therefore I came to seek
You, whom I know so little—yet I know
That you alone can save him. Long ago
They hunted you from Athens. Is that hard,
O Daedalus, to pardon? What reward—
Ah there is none that you would stoop to take!"
"Except that I had done it for your sake"
He answered simply. Silent for a space
They sat, while eagerly she watched his face,
Puckered with thinking. "Know you what you ask?"
He said. "Think you this youth will leave his task?

That though I gave you now his prison's key,
Flung wide its door, he would take your liberty?
What then? If he meets that Dweller in the Tomb?—
Listen. What lies within the mountain's womb,
High up the peak of Iuktas, none can know.
When first I came to Crete, long years ago,
I hewed that web of backward-winding ways
For Minos—that inextricable maze,
Named of the Sacred Axe, whence none return,
Save Minos. Yet not all my craft could learn
For what strange guest that stranger house was wrought."
Darkly he paused, as fearing his own thought
Might peep from out his eyes. Then musingly—
"That riddle's end this youth from oversea
May find at last. But now, from us, what aid?
Lest he fall weaponless, a dagger-blade;
Lest he be chained, a file; and lest that cave
With its black winding entrails be his grave,
Something to trace his own steps back to day—
All this is easy." Yet once more his eyes
Hovered on hers in flickering surmise:
"Think well. Strange things may come of this
        night's work,
And not alone to what weird shape may lurk
High up Mount Iuktas. Think—the Lord of Crete,
When sinks to-morrow's sun, will set his feet,

Likewise, within that darkness—and his throne,
With all the land of Cnossus, may atone
For what this night we do." She hid her brow
Deep in her hands a moment, moaning low;
And then—"I love my father. But this land—
I hate it. And if all its fortunes stand
Built on the bones of murder, let it fall!
Give me the dagger." Outside, gaunt and tall
Under the sleepless silence of the stars
One swaying cypress tapped the window-bars.
She stared across the darkness, wondering
How calm her pulses beat—no guilty thing
She felt, but like a shape of dream, the while
The old man from his chest drew forth a file,
Fumbling and peering, then a fisher's line.
"On this poor thread," he smiled "though it be fine,
Men's lives shall hang. Let him hitch fast its hook
In the cave's mouth; and then down every crook
And twisting turn pay out upon his way
This, that shall lead him back at last to day."
Then "Icarus!" he called; and drowsy-eyed,
With insolent mouth, to his old father's side
A tall lad came. But Ariadne said
"No, no, he shall not take them. On my head,
Not his, shall fall this madness. And to me
That prison-door will open easily,

Being Minos' daughter. Quick, for I must be gone.
Before the first cock crows, all must be done."
She caught her cloak about her. Then, more slow:
"Upon my head, I said. Yet well I know
What doom may fall on yours. What can I say?
How can my helpless gratitude repay?
Why have you dared this folly? Why have I,
Who move as in a dream, not knowing why?"
He smiled—"Do you think, then, life so dear to me,
Who, save my blindworm's curiosity,
Have nothing left to live for. I am old.
And what is love to me? And what is gold?
To conquer things, to break their stubborn will,
Wrench out of them their secrets—these are still
Some means to make the heavy hours and slow
Pass swiftly, yet forget how swift they go;
Dreaming of all the marvels they shall bring
To men, long after our brief fluttering,
When all the earth shall serve, and sea, and sky,
Our children's children. Ah, how happily
The world shall live when you and I are dead!
Why help you now? Because that golden head
Brings back lost memories of home to me,
Of the hills of Hellas that I shall not see
For ever? Or because I gave my youth
Too passionately to serve not love, but truth,

And grieve too late I made no heart my own?—
Ah, dull and heavy grows the head, alone!
But Icarus scorns" (he smiled) "my talking tongue,
For the young hate to think the old were young.
Go, the Gods help you, as I have striven to do!
If you love him—(do not flush)—ah then, be true
To the world's end. And do not fear for me
Your father's rage, though Crete and all the sea
Tremble before him; though this head be grey,
Time has not stolen all its wits away."
Soft as a flitting shadow down the hill
She vanished, and that lonely room grew still
Save for the night-owl's whimper; in his fire,
Regretting vanished youth and vain desire,
The old man gazed; but hurrying through the gloom
She passed the palace-gate, and reached the room
Where sprawled the guard asleep, save two that played
At dice by the blood-red embers. Then she bade
Their captain lead her where the stranger lay,
So proudly, that he durst not say her nay;
Guessing her father sent her, so to wring
By fair words from the prince some secret thing
Before he died; nor thought to disbelieve
Her who had danced with Death but yestereve
To save her father from this stranger's spear.
So in the straw, with voices in his ear

And lamplight in his eyes, Theseus awoke.
And now they stood alone. Yet neither spoke;
Until he cried—"Have you come to triumph again,
O cold blue eyes? For this, then, have I lain
This last night of my life shut up alone,
Cut off from those I loved? The heart was stone
That ordered it. Not you? Surely not you?"
She trembled; then from out her mantle drew
The dark-blue-gleaming dagger and the file.
Watching her fair grave face, with a sudden smile
He raised his chained wrists towards her. Silently
She knelt and stretched his chain across her knee;
Then for a little space no sound was heard
Save the snarl of bitten bronze. Without a word,
He gazed upon those steadfast downcast eyes,
That firm-set mouth, while in his mute surprise,
Just as in some rich garden a fountain throws
Its rainbow spray this way and that, as blows
The veering breeze, so swift his musings bent
A hundred ways, to fathom what intent
Lay hid behind that white, unflinching brow.
Breathless, she rested. Then "What brings you now,"
Low-voiced he said "who sprang so unafraid
Last night to save your father, when my blade
Pricked at his breast?" She answered "Is it strange
To pity? Well I knew no threat could change

His purpose. Ah, why waste this idle breath?—
Could I sit still and watch death breeding death?"
Dimly across their faces, to and fro,
The shadows danced. "Yet" said he "I must go
To face my fate, to-morrow. If I live,
It shall not be a shamefaced fugitive,
Come empty home from Crete." She bowed her head,
While at her heart clutched the cold hand of dread:
"Yes, Theseus. That at least I knew too well,
Though little else I know; who cannot tell
Why I betray for you my father's land
As if I blindly must; nor understand
Why now I care no longer though the price
Of the Gods' anger for their sacrifice
Profaned perhaps through you, should overthrow
Cnossus from its foundation. Better so,
Than stand the slaughter-house of innocence!
But listen. When at dawn they lead you hence
High up the crags of Iuktas to that cave,
That gateway of the kingdom of the grave,
Make fast within its mouth this fisher's line,
And through your fingers let its length untwine
Down through the winding gloom. Then if again—"
With a half-stifled sob she seized his chain
And her swift feverish fingers toiled once more
To sever it. But with a laugh he tore

The half-cut links in sunder, and instead
His hands were round her wrists. White as the dead,
With a low cry she turned her face away,
Glad, helpless, weak within his arms she lay.
Then as he felt her warmth against his breast,
Her golden head so wearily at rest,
Tenderness, and desire, and gratitude,
Passionate admiration, hope renewed,
Rose, as a sudden storm across a hill,
Melting its crags to cloud, to bind and blind his will.
But backward from his grasp she slipped and cried
"Soon Love forgets her that forgets her pride—
Yet if you die—what then were pride to me!
Is it my empty pride I would keep free,
Or love I dread to lose? O foolish heart,
What matter, when we kiss only to part
For ever?" Desperately, she seized his hands
And pressed them to her brow, as one that stands
Not knowing if he wakes or lies asleep,
Whether he longs to laugh or fears to weep.
And then—"O Theseus, this is madness—blind—
Think, think—(ah how to bear it!)—if you find
Your way to the light again, how will you flee
This angry land?" "Send one you trust," said he,
"Down to the port, to whisper in the ear
Of the Black Ship's master—let him linger here,

Caulking some leak, until three days are past;
And let him set a man high up his mast
Nightly to watch towards Iuktas. On its height
If he sees a beacon-flame, ere dawn is light,
I will be with him. Then, though it rain or hail,
Let him look to beat his way with oar and sail
Out of the road of Cnossus, ere the day
Calls all the keels of Crete to track their prey.
And now—fear not! This day I looked to die,
I dreamed that Pallas Athene passed me by—
Her cold eyes would not heed me, her deaf ears
     hear my cry;
As if in Crete before the ancient throne
Of the Mother of the Gods, her power were grown
Helpless to save—but now, ah now, I see
She sends another in her stead to me."
She smiled—"O foolish tongue, O flattering breath,
Will you yet flatter in the face of Death?"
But he caught her hands and cried "To-night, to-night,
Or else to-morrow, if that beacon-light
Shines over Cnossus—will no other eye,
O Ariadne, search the midnight sky?"
She met his eyes with eyes as true as day,
Trusting within his hand her white hand lay—
"You are bold, Theseus. You do not fear to crave
Too much of Fortune. Yet she loves the brave,

They say. Am I your Fortune? Yes, you smile.
And yet, ah think, how much you ask the while
Of me who yesterday still knew you not.
Though you forget, think you I have forgot
In one short night the home of all my days,
To follow an unknown face on unknown ways—
Although this land of Cnossus, this dark race
Be but half mine? From far, from windy Thrace,
My mother came to sleep at Minos' side,
His slave (ah, you guessed not that!) and not his bride;
Though her father once was king in that wild land
Where round the swirling Hebrus the peaks of
    Haemus stand.
So half I hate this land of weasel priests,
Blessing the bulls that gore men at their feasts,
This land of painted loves and scented lusts.
And yet—my father—he has none he trusts
But me; none else that loves him—long ago
My mother died; and then—(too well you know)—
His best-loved son, in Athens. Now, alone,
That heart too just has hardened on his throne
To all but me, but me—shall I turn it to stone?
And yet to-night . . . O Theseus, harsh is youth,
And love that would die for love, yet knows no ruth
Though all life else should perish. Ah, dear heart,
All this may be a dream. Now, ere we part,

I kiss you once farewell. Go—think of me
As living only with your memory
Through these black hours to come; and let the
    thought
Of what our love may be, keep true and taut
Your courage—O my love, may it keep mine,
Until the hills see your red beacon shine,
Till—Oh your love is true, you have not lied?—
We meet as day is breaking, beneath the Black
    Ship's side."
At those last words a stab ran through his heart,
The mists that veiled his memory fell apart,
Once more he saw that little lonely isle,
Aegle's dark eyes, her sad foreboding smile,
Once more he heard her words—"In Heaven there sits
Another Goddess whose light favour flits
From face to face." So short a while—and now
The lips of Ariadne touched his brow.
But at her touch again his blood took fire
And in his heart he cried, blind with desire,
"It is too late. She is too beautiful.
Ah, God, I cannot lose her. O poor fool!—
And yet what matter? I shall die to-day,
And all is over. Or, if I hew our way
Back to the light, why, it is sweet to live
And, owing me life, my old love will forgive

Her fickle lover." Yet his heart was wrung,
As in a last embrace they kissed and clung,
To see the guilelessness in those clear eyes,
To feel his own feet meshed in a web of lies.
She tore herself away—then in the door
Faltered, and turned her face towards him once
     more,
Lifting above her head the lamp nigh spent,
In one last look, so tender, so intent,
As if she would have stamped unchangeably
His look upon her vision, and then see
No more for ever. Harshly the great door slammed
Between them, and the grim guard stooping rammed
The bronze bolt home. In the dawn's first
     glimmering grey
On the benches in the guard-room where they lay
Sprawling, the Carian spearmen half awoke
And on their elbows stared as her rich cloak
Swept fluttering past and vanished in the gloom.
She climbed the stair, fled on from room to room;
Far down the shadowy palace-passages
The painted beasts of fresco and of frieze
Seemed as if they too stirred in that dim light
Of a new day. She crossed a courtyard. White
Above the hills like some curved edge of war
The sickle-moon arose, while faint and far

Trumpets of cock-crow called the dawn to arms
And the keen cold breath of daybreak in the palms
Whirled high their sworded leaves. There lay at last
Her own still room—so still, it seemed to cast
A half-reproach upon her with its peace,
Its quiet welcome, its faithful memories
Of childish days when love was but a flower,
And grief ungrown, and life a singing bower
That had not heard the axe, nor felt the gale.
And now... Sadly she watched beneath its veil
Of tossed black curls the little Phaedra's face
Breathing untroubled, pillowed on the grace
Of one white arm. She tried to sleep. In vain—
Too loud her heart, too tight the band of pain
About her breast. Then rose the tramp of feet,
The muffled clash of arms. Far up the street
She heard them pass. Then, hoarse and harsh and strong,
Through the red dawn rang out the Slaying Song
Of the marching priests of Cnossus, till the flute
Died wailing in the distance, and was mute,
And the fierce clang of cymbals up the hill
Grew faint and fainter, and the dusk was still,
But for its chirping birds. And yet no sleep—
She seemed to see, with heart too full to weep,
That long procession thread the Southern Gate,
The guard, the captives, the black chair of state,

Of gold and cypress-wood, that hid the King
As if it were to his own burying
They bore the Lord of Cnossus; then, behind,
The chanting priests. Upwards she saw them wind
Through olive-grove and vineyard, sad and slow—
Wondering the little goatherds watched them go
And ceased their piping. Then the mountain-track,
The parching climb and, far off, looming black
That mouth of Death—she moaned. Too grim
    to bear
The stillness grew. She rose, she bowed in prayer
Not to the Gods of Crete, but those of old
Her mother taught—Ares, that loves the bold,
And Artemis, that hears the maiden's cry,
Mistress of all wild things that run or swim or fly,
And Dionysus, Lord of ecstasy,
Lord of all spirits tameless, all souls free,
Who breaks kings' sceptres, and grey custom's chain,
And bids the slave rise up, the conquered fight again.
Her maidens came and clad her for the day
In its black garb of mourning; untouched lay
The sacred bread they brought, unheeded whined
Laelaps her hound. Then softly from behind
Crept Phaedra, whispering "Quick!—what have you
    planned?"
But Ariadne seized her sister's hand

And kissed her mouth to silence; from the room,
Leaving her maidens laughing round their loom,
She hurried, while with eager questioning air
The child gazed up at her, and down the stair,
Then in the court bade harness to her car
Her sleek grey mules. The grooms ran to unbar
The great bronze gateway—down the winding street
She drove through Cnossus, while the men of Crete
All clad in black (in her heart the thought rose dim
Theseus was dead, and all men mourned for him)
Made way before her. In the market-place
The buzzing gossips paused to watch her face,
Girls at their lovers' arms pulled jealously,
And old wives, hand on hip, craning to see
Her beauty, at her sadness shook their heads
And muttered—"Ay, 'tis too long ere she weds,
And she so fair. King Minos should long since
Have found a husband for her—some proud prince
Of Phaestus or Eleusarna." But their praise
She heard not, as with hard and tearless gaze
She stared before her where the white road ran
Out through the Northern Gateway's ancient span
Seaward betwixt the olives. Strangely dear
Even its dry dust seemed, to think that here
But yesterday he passed—how could it be
But yesterday? It seemed eternity.

103

Could her love be but a day-old infant yet?
So swift to grow! So swift, too, to forget?
Ah no—not that—not ever! Blue and white,
With all its myriad masts, before her sight
The haven opened. Far from the rest, alone,
The Black Ship lay; as some bull overthrown
In battle, lays his black bulk sullenly
Aloof, and watches from beneath his tree
The happy herd along the riverside.
But even as she gazed, the halyards cried
And the black sail crawled flapping up its mast.
For in the darkness, ere the night was passed,
A horseman armed had ridden within hail
And bidden them not linger, but set sail
In the name of the Lord of Cnossus. White she grew
And stooping lashed her mules until they flew,
Sparks round their feet, down the steep cobbled way,
Whirled to the left and flashed along the bay.
A spear-shot short she reined them from the ship,
And said to Phaedra, finger laid to lip,
"Quick, little sister, run! For three nights yet,
Say to the master, let him wait and set
Watch for the glare of a beacon-flame by night
On Iuktas; then—before the morning's light—
Look he be ready to flee the Cretan shore.
Let him say his timbers leak; and if, before,

They bid him hence, tell him to show this ring
Graved with the griffin of the Cretan King."
Then, as the little maid ran, glad and proud
To share in such a secret, calling loud
To the Greek seamen, low beneath her breath
To herself she said "And this, perhaps, is death,
If once my father knew—" and suddenly
The heart within her leapt to think that she
Should live or die with Theseus, by one fate,
And from her soul, it seemed, slipped half its weight.
But now the child ran laughing back. She swept
The shore with one swift glance. The harbour slept,
Only an old man by the Black Ship scanned
Her face, his sharp eyes sheltered with his hand,
As if he doubted her—yet found too fair
That face for falsehood. Downwards through the air
The black sail fluttered. Then along the shore
Slowly she drove her mules, with heart too sore
To turn back home—how should she sit and while
The crawling hours away, with hollow smile
Masking her anguish? Where a streamlet danced
Down through its plane-trees' shade, while gaily glanced
The sunbeams on its ripples through the boughs,
'Mid the lush grass she left her beasts to browse
And climbed a rock and seaward gazed alone.
High up the sea-mews wailed, and on the stone

The flickering lizards watched her, unafraid,
So still she sat—remembering, while they played
Free in the sunlight, wrists that wore a chain,
Eyes in a cavern's darkness that looked for light in vain.
Below, with some old song upon her tongue
That immemorial nurseries had sung,
The little Phaedra gathered shells; or gay
And chattering by Ariadne lay,
To eat brown bread and olives. Out at sea
Thera and Ios and faint Anaphe
On the far skyline slowly changed their hue,
As onward evening stole, from grey to blue.
Then sick with a nameless dread of coming night
She rose and turned her glad mules homeward—light
Up the long hill they flew, while the white dust
Smoked high behind them. Bliss it was to thrust
Thought for a moment from her, as with feet
Firm set she lashed them up the Cnossian street.
No black draped now the hall; high on the dais,
Feasting her kindred sat; with curious gaze
They watched her as, unwilling, to her place
She came. Her food half choked her. At her face
With a half-smile glanced pale Pasiphae,
Then plunged in dreams again, while windily
The dark Deucalion at the table's head
Boasted of bulls' necks shattered, men's blood shed,

106

By his strong arm before the gathered eyes
Of Crete; and Acacallis with low sighs,
Heeding him not, dreamed of a vanished day,
While an old harper sang the ancient lay
How God Himself on the blest Syrian shore
Was once made flesh, and in a bull's shape bore
Agenor's daughter from the meadows where
She gathered lilies, through those meadows bare
In which nought but the white foam comes to flower,
To the coasts of Crete, that so the royal power
Of Cnossus from her womb might come to birth.
But the young Catreus cried "What is the worth
Of such old threadbare tales of long ago!
Sing a new song—sing us of things we know
A song we know not. Let the dead praise the dead!"
The old man sighed; then with a shaken head
Chanted how Minos sailed to levy war
Against King Nisus, Lord of Megara;
And how the princess Scylla, from the gate
Watching the battle, grew so passionate
For love of Minos that she sheared away
The purple lock in which his magic lay
From her own father's temples, as he slept,
And through the darkness of the armies crept
To Minos' tent, and cried "O love, I bring
To a king's feet the fortunes of a king."

But Minos loathed that gift of treachery
And, sailing home in triumph, through the sea
From his ship's sternpost dragged her till she died.
Then, as the minstrel ceased, on every side
The shadowy hall lay hushed, for all men knew
This was no minstrel's dream, but bitter-true.
And Ariadne flushed, to think that she,
She too was such a traitress. Fixedly,
As she glanced up, again the bright, brown eye
Of her step-mother watched her, as on high
With hardly a flicker of his bright, brown wing
The hawk hangs o'er his quarry. Murmuring
In her smooth voice, "Why then so sad," she said,
"My Ariadne, when the wine runs red?
Grief should have died at sunset, with our fast,
Seeing that on Iuktas, ere this night is past,
Our Lord shall rise again, again reborn,
To ride in triumph through Cnossus on the morn.
Now on the Mount of God our enemies
Go to their death—away with mournful eyes!"
Darkly she dwelt on Ariadne's look
At that word "death"—but in a voice that shook
With a child's shrill passionate anger, Phaedra cried
"O mother, why be glad if he has died—
That brave young stranger! Ah, if I were King,
I would give him life, not death, and a gold ring

To wed dear Ariadne, so that peace
Might be between us and the kings of Greece.
As for the Dweller in the Cavern, he
Should feed himself, or else go starve, for me!"
Deep fell the hush, while Ariadne trod
On Phaedra's foot, and with an angry nod
Deucalion growled "Hush, little fool, go play!
Tempt not the gods with evil words, lest they
Send evil deeds in answer. As for him,
This stranger that you praise so, smooth and trim,
Would that last night we had grappled longer there,
Till I had snapped his neck. But you, beware!
Remember Scylla's end. So perish those
That dare to smile upon their country's foes!
Go learn of Ariadne—long may thrive
Crete, with such hearts to breed us, and to wive!"
She read, even as he praised her, in his face
The dark, hid passions of his mother's race,
Grown hot with wine. "Easy indeed," she said,
With a low laugh, "for you to drink him dead,
Being so pot-valiant! Yet even that might buy
A braver name than making children cry!"
Then clasping Phaedra's hand before them all,
Without a word, scornful and pale and tall,
She pushed her gold seat from her, and passed from
     out the hall.

Then, when her sister slept, with flying feet
She gained the roof—her heart nigh ceased to beat,
As first she looked towards Iuktas, with delight
Beyond all hope, for one faint twinkling light
Gleamed from its crest—alas, 'twas but a star.
Cool on her fevered forehead from afar
The night-wind breathed, while slowly to and fro
One lonely poplar nodded, and below
From the unseen river the frogs' gurgling glee
Took up its night-long mirthless mockery.
An owl wailed through the gloom; the city slept;
Hopeless, alone, she bowed her face and wept,
Seeing how blank the future, dead the past,
Remembering what sorrow overcast
Her mother's days, far from her native land—
How on such evenings she too used to stand
To feel upon her face the north wind blow
Cool from far Haemus with its ageless snow;
Till all life seemed so bitter, from the wall
She measured with her eye the headlong fall
To death's forgetfulness. High overhead
Watched the cold stars that still would watch her dead,
Unpitying, unheeding. Far away
Awoke a nightingale—so sweet, so gay,
She strained to listen: for it seemed to cry
How fair are all things living, though they die,

How new are all things, though our youth grows old,
How cruel is life, yet how it loves the bold—
All who amid the anguish of past days,
The dread of days to come, learn but to praise
More passionately, to feel with keener sense
The brave, brief beauty of life's transience;
Whose hearts in secret sing from hill to hill,
Whose song no darkness save of death can still.
She said "I have loved at least. It will have been!"
But as she said it, lo, a first pale sheen,
A quivering light, a round red Cyclops' eye
On the forehead of Mount Iuktas. With a cry
She swayed—and then, forgetting all her fears,
With all her wild heart hammering in her ears,
Swift from the roof to her own room she fled,
Flung herself down and sobbing hid her head
Deep in the pillows, until Phaedra cried,
Waking, "O Ariadne, has he died?"
"No, no. The beacon burns. He comes—comes now,
My love, my love." Silent she leant her brow
Upon her hand, and thought; then rising threw
Round her a cloak, and on her finger drew
Her mother's ring, and in her bosom laid
A Cretan dagger—down its golden blade
There flew a swan of silver. Wistfully
She gazed around the room that she would see

III

No more for ever, after all these years,
And stooping kissed through a blind mist of tears
Phaedra, who wept and pleaded, clinging tight,
To come with her—"Ah would, dear heart, you might!
Remember me. And if they ask you, say
I rose to hunt alone at break of day.
Farewell, my sweet." But Phaedra, tearful, smiled—
"Ah, I shall come some day. I shall run wild.
They shall not cage me here. And then beware!
I shall make your Greek prince love me. Oh take care—
Be happy, Ariadne." So she crept
Out through the darkness to the room where slept
Her father; there, upon the empty bed
She pinned one curl cut from her golden head
To the hard pillow—he might curse her, yet
Though unforgiven, she would not forget.
Then with her hood pulled close about her face
Down the dark street, through the gaunt market-place
She stole, while at her heel Laelaps the hound
Trotted with ears pricked gaily; not a sound—
The night lay dead, save when a cart piled high
With country-fare for the morrow's feast creaked by.
Across the olive-boughs the stars shone down
Like silver berries. Deep the harbour-town
Slept, and the beaked ships by the water's edge
In their long rows, like sea-birds on a ledge

Above the sleepless surges. Through the blank
Of gloom, as if some mighty creature drank,
Weltered the hollow lapping of the sea;
Else all was silence save when stealthily
A harbour-rat ran past, or nodding slow
The palm-leaves in the star-light whispered low
"Ah, leave not the sweet South!" So dark and still
Even the Black Ship lay, a sudden chill
Of terror stabbed her to the heart—had she
But dreamed she saw what she so longed to see,
Gleaming high up Mount Iuktas? One by one
The dull hours dragged, and night was nearly done.
On a sudden Laelaps growled—athwart the gloom,
Ghost-like, she saw a stumbling figure loom,
Bearing a woman's body, as if dead.
"Theseus!" she whispered. Never a word he said,
But caught her hand and stood there, breathing fast;
Behind, more shadows thickened; then at last
He whistled low. From the ship an answer cried.
Nearing, they saw dark figures round her side,
Backs bent and strong arms straining; down the shore
To the black water's bosom with a roar
She plunged, as smoothly as an otter slips
Down through the rustling river-reeds, and dips
His glossy body in the gurgling deep.
They swarmed aboard—the oars leapt out, to sweep

The mirrored stars from the still water's breast
And whirl them in dancing eddies east and west.
Then, as they cleared the shadow of the hill,
Fluttering aloft the sail began to fill
Before the breath of dawn. Sharp from the snow
Of Ida now it blew, while morn's red glow
Climbed smouldering up the east. Behind them fell
The harbour-mouth; the home where she would dwell
No more for ever, faded as a dream
From eyes awakened by the daylight's gleam.
She thought of the house her childhood's feet had trod;
And how her father from the face of God
Would come that day in triumph—and, when he came,
Find she had left him loneliness and shame.
Almost her heart failed, as she watched the shore
Grow faint; not knowing he would nevermore
Feel grief or shame or loneliness henceforth.
But now the sea-swell caught them from the north—
The bronze beak plunging gashed the smooth round back
Of each green roller, while upon their track
The south wind freshened and white whirled the spray.
Then, as she watched, it seemed from far away
A great cry rose, and through the darkened town
Wild lights, like marsh-fires, flitted up and down
From house to house. A warm hand touched her hand—
Grave-eyed behind her she saw Theseus stand.

IV

κᾰλήν τ’ Ἀριάδνην
κούρην Μίνωος ὀλοόφρονος, ἥν ποτε Θησεὺς
ἐκ Κρήτης ἐς γουνὸν Ἀθηνάων ἱεράων
ἦγε μέν, οὐδ’ ἀπόνητο.

                    Homer, "Odyssey."

And lovely Ariadne,
Grim-hearted Minos' child, whom Theseus brought
From Crete to the verge of the sacred soil of Athens,
Yet had no joy of her.

IV

SLOWLY between them and the coasts of Crete
They stretched a waste of waters; hills her feet
Had known so well—now stern and strange and grey
Their seaward faces watched her on her way.
Then old Euaemon bade the steersman run
Eastward behind green Dia, so to shun
Avengers out of Cnossus; till at last,
If the wind veered, they might wheel north-
    westward past
Casos and Cos and up the Sporades.
But Theseus called—"No! Steer before the breeze
Due north for Naxos and Cape Sunium."
Then the old man cried "Oh mad! Would you have
    them come
Dead on our track! We must dodge them like a hare.
They can outsail us. Saw you not the glare
Of torches lit already as we fled?"
But Theseus with a dark smile shook his head—
"Fear not; the men of Crete have other things
To fill their thoughts through this day's revellings."
Then in the stern by Ariadne's side
He turned to look at her and, lo, there died

That smile and on his face a shadow lay
As from her hand he drew his hand away.
"What means" she thought "that look?" An
        unknown dread
Caught at her throat. "O love, my love," he said
"Can you forgive me? Not for me to hold
That hand—will you loathe my sight, when all
        is told?"
She caught his wrist, and cried "What have you done?"
He drew it back, he looked aside to shun
Her eager face. "Your father—" "Yes," she cried
"Is there aught ill with him?" Low he replied
"Nothing. No ill can touch him any more."
"Not dead? Not dead! Why spoke you not before?
How could it happen? Theseus, not by you!
Ah, had you loved me, had you but been true,
You had remembered as you raised your hand,
How once I saved him—would have seen me stand,
Though far away, to guard once more his heart.
And I that armed you—I too played my part!
I too have killed him!" Dumb, she bowed her head.
"O love, I did not even know," he said,
"I did not know him. If I must lose you, still
Forgive me, ah forgive my blinded will."
She met his eyes—"Though it be Hell to hear,
Tell me the truth. Then rest—for, O my dear,

118

Two nights you have not slept. Look how they sleep,
Your comrades, in a weariness so deep
They lie like death. You must sleep; for my sake."
"Ah Ariadne, I shall lie awake
Till you forgive me. Listen. In the dark
We left the gate of Cnossus; gaunt and stark
The hills rose round us; then the morning heat
On that bare mountain-path began to beat,
Blinding, upon us from the white limestone.
The horned wild goats, the kestrel soaring lone
Above us mocked our plodding misery.
My broken chain I kept hid close to me
Under my cloak; but I durst not slip the file
To those beside me, though we lay awhile
Breathless, beside a spring, beneath a pine,
For some had fainted. Black bread dipped in wine
They flung us—and then onward up the crag.
The sun was sinking, and we scarce could drag
Our torn feet further, when at last we came
To a rifted rock. Lit by three torches' flame
King Minos passed within its echoing mouth,
While we, bowed down with weariness and drouth,
Lay in the opening, watching out at sea
Thera and Ios and far Anaphe,
And dreaming how from thence a ship might sail
With the wind of dawn and ere the evening hail

The warders of Phalerum. Then the sun
Sank—two black eunuchs carried, one by one,
The weeping maidens in and washed the dust
From their tired bodies and upon them thrust
Bride-robes of purple and a bridal veil,
While two priests sprinkled on our faces pale
Their holy water and hung round each head
Wild mountain-flowers, white lilies of the dead,
And round each neck, emblem of men that die
To live again, a golden butterfly.
Then through the twilight rose the evening star—
Into the dark they drove us; winding far
Down mazy passages before us went
With torch in hand to light the black descent
A spearman, and a second strode behind—
Yet softly through my hand the clue untwined.
We came to a shrine, deep in the mountain's womb,
With sacred axes glittering through its gloom;
And there the Mother stood, shaped as She stands
In Minos' hall, with coiled snakes in Her hands,
On Her head the triple crown, and bare Her breast,
And at Her feet lay carved a lion at rest.
Again the darkness swallowed us, again
The blind ways twisted like a tangled skein,
Until again a glimmer of candleshine
And, lo, we stood within a second shrine

120

Before the Goddess. But now Her dark face smiled
And at Her naked breast She nursed a child,
While a wild goat beside Her fed its young.
Then, when before Her too the priests had sung
A wailing chant, through the blind gloom we
    came
To a third chapel, bright with tapers' flame,
Where facing Her there stood with arms upthrown
To worship Her, that child to boyhood grown.
There too they prayed, and passed, till last of all
Out of the darkness to a mightier hall
We came, where the Mother of Life stood carved
    no more,
But round the rock-hewn walls, from roof to floor,
Dull the light gleamed on great sarcophagi
Of polished granite, where had come to lie
The Lords of Cnossus in their last long pride
From untold generations side by side.
But in the midst upon a marble throne
There sat a shape of horror, all alone—
A shape bull-headed. At its feet glowed red
A horned altar and, beyond, a bed
Lay bright with flowers. There after worship done
They ranged us by the wall and, one by one,
With bull's hide bound our feet—then suddenly
The hall lay empty, nought was left to see

Save the tapers burning in that windless gloom,
Till all at once with a deep hollow boom
The bronze door slammed upon us. Then my hair
Prickled, my mouth went dry—before us there
From its throne of polished stone that thing of
    dread
Had risen. Slowly towards us turned its head—
A sword flashed in its hand. I slipped my chain
And with your dagger hacked the thongs in twain
That bound my feet. To see one victim free
The monster started; while it stared at me,
I sundered too the bonds about the feet
Of Euthycles my comrade. Then the Thing
Bellowed aloud, half man-like; echoing
Among the stony coffins of the dead
And down those trackless corridors it sped,
That desperate cry, as though it would recall
The vanished guards. But still and silent all
As its dead kings lay that dim underworld.
I stooped to free a third. But swift it whirled
The sword above its head and rushed at me.
Lightly I slipped aside—the Thing could see
But blindly in that half-light. Then I cried
To the rest to free their feet and on each side
Harass him as they might with wrists fast bound.
The creature paused—I saw him look around

Uncertain, should he rush on us once more
Or edge along the wall and gain the door.
Then straight at me he leapt; I wrapped my cloak
Close round my arm and warded off the stroke,
Though to the bone it cut—my point came out
Through his right shoulder. Then with a wild shout
Sprang Euthycles upon him, but he thrust
My comrade to the heart, and in the dust
Hurled off two others, as a wild boar flings
From his black-bristled cheek the hound that clings,
And reached the wall and sideways to the right
Edged facing us. Then lost indeed the fight,
If in the dark the Thing escaped our gaze
And held us trapped within that trackless maze;
And yet—so long his sword—approach him near
We durst not; as the dogs about a deer
Leap snapping round, yet dread his antlers' length.
I sought some missile that might maim his strength,
But only those dark coffins of the dead
Faced me, each way I turned. Faster he fled—
He had reached the corner—then I spied his throne;
I sprang upon it, I wrenched free the stone—
Now he had reached the door—it held—it gave,
Through it the darkness loomed, too late to save.
For through the air that weight of marble flashed—
Beneath his own proud throne he swayed and crashed.

I seized his horned head—it came away
Loose in my hand—O love, before me lay,
Among those ancient kings of all his race,
Your father." With a sob she hid her face.
Yet round his wrist her white hands stole once more
And gripped it hard; dim lay the Cretan shore
Behind them now. "O love, you do not fear
Blood-guilt?" he whispered. Slow she shook her head—
"Where did you leave him?" "On that bed, flower-bright
As a young bride's, till the last candlelight
Should gutter out and hide him there at last,
One with the darkness of the ancient past.
I pondered whether by him we should lay
Euthycles also; there to sleep away
Their last long night, the slayer by the slain.
Yet I feared the priests in vengeance might profane
His body, and his spirit find no rest,
Its dust dishonoured. So when they had dressed
My wound, and filed their fetters, by the door
We sought the clue and slowly stumbling bore
Our dead back to the light. Two fires we found,
With priests and guards sitting and laughing round
Against the morrow's riot and revelry—
Forth from the gloom we leapt with one fierce cry,
Ere they could arm, and three we slaughtered there,
The rest we hunted headlong, stripped and bare,

Down the sheer blackness of the mountain. Then
On a crag that faced the sea, above the glen
We piled a hasty pyre and in its flame
Laid Euthycles and three times called his name
While the red blaze rose roaring through the night.
But long we dared not wait—on that bleak height
We heaved above his ashes one great stone
And there on Iuktas left him lying alone.
That flame you saw, O love. The rest is told."
Her hand in his, she watched how past them rolled
Wave after wave, and up the northern sky
Once more the sea-girt Cyclades rose high
While in the south the peak of Iuktas fell,
With its stone face, behind the deep's long swell;
As if with it the memory of guilt
Sank, and in that blue sea the dark blood spilt
Were washed away for ever. Low she said
"Not yours the fault, my Theseus. On his head
His own doom fell. Your life he would not spare:
Fate spared not him. No shielding hand was there
That second time, my father. Do you think
It strange that I can bear this, and not shrink
With horror that my father did such things?—
Ah, I am hardened against shudderings.
Dear heart, I knew too much, though never this;
I knew too well that there is no abyss

Of filth and infamy men have not trod
At a priest's word, to do the will of God.
And yet so strange—the hand that smoothed my hair
Could kill men helpless in a wild beast's lair;
The heart that judged, though harshly, yet so well
On the throne of Cnossus, could enact this Hell—
Horned like a monstrous beast, till like a beast
    he fell!
O Theseus, what are the gods? And what are we
That worship them for their iniquity?
No god at least, save Death, shall bid us part.
But now, Oh sleep, weary and o'erwatched heart!
Let me lay you to your slumber like my child."
Then at her feet he stretched himself; she smiled,
Too fond herself to sleep, as, like the sea,
That strong chest heaved and sank so peacefully,
Till the day waned, and to the Cyclades
They came—like sheep across the grass-green seas
At pasture, herded by the westering sun.
By Pholegandros, then, they turned to run,
'Twixt Sikinos and Ios, to the strait
That parts Paros from Naxos. Eve grew late.
They beached their ship high up the Naxian shore
In a lone bay, and kindled fire, and bore
Goat's flesh and wine to land; then loud and long,
Half-mad with joy, they feasted, till their song

Woke all the echoes hidden in the hills,
As if the unseen nymphs of woods and rills
And shouting satyrs, reeling in their mirth,
Danced in the dark, for spring come back to earth.
Only on Ariadne's heart there fell
A silent sorrow—still she saw too well
That empty chamber and her golden tress,
Pinned there in vain to soothe his loneliness
That lay now in a lonelier resting-place;
Round her she felt a strange, a younger race,
Braver than came of Crete, gayer than dwelt in
      Thrace—
Yet all unknown; strangely their watching eyes
Followed her with their restless, sharp surmise.
One face, beyond the rest, seemed bent on her,
As sad as those were gay; too sad to stir,
Except when Theseus spoke—a woman's face,
Dark-lashed, not beautiful, but with a grace
That troubled Ariadne; deep and dumb
Those Sibyl's eyes, and dark with ills to come.
Then, as the wine went round and yet more gay
Rang shout and laughter, that face slipped away;
And after a little Theseus rose and passed
Out of the firelight. By a spring at last
He came on her, that softly murmuring fell
From a cleft rock—"You are sad. And why, too well,

Aegle, I know. Yet surely life is sweet?
Shame ties my tongue, to think how soon my feet
Have fallen in golden Aphrodite's snare—
Too true you spoke, sad heart, too wise you were!
And yet she saved us." "Would not I have died,
Oh, gladly—with a smile—for you!" she cried;
And shuddering was silent. With a groan
"I know," he said "I know: yet who can rule
His heart? Each one of us is but the fool
Of Eros—Love's poor puppet. Easier turn
The torrent back than bid man's blood not burn.
Would you have me lie? Would you I played a part—
Gave you as yours, what was another's heart?
Could such love make us happy?" Silently
She shook her head—then moaned "Will you—will she
Find happiness in this? O faithless one,
Not long to wait, till my revenge is won!
And yet what help?—though I drank her heart's
        blood raw,
Would mine find ease? O love, I love you more
Than life. But Love, like Death, has stony ears
To prayer; yet Death, though not Love, dries our tears."
"Ah but the dead return not; Love can rise
Fresh from his grave. Oh yet be brave, be wise!
I loved you. That is over—not untrue.
A dower to make the proudest proud to woo,

O Aegle, shall be yours." "Ah no," she cried
"For shame, for shame! Far better flung aside
Than sold!" Then with a sob she turned and fled
Into the darkness; and with hanging head
And heavy heart to the laughter by the fire
He came again, and the face of his desire.
Pensive she sat, with a sad questioning look—
And yet with such a lonely longing shook
His voice, so wildly yearned in his worn eyes
His passion, deep within her she felt rise
A sudden rush of pity—"Ah indeed"
To herself she said "I will not fail his need.
Here he shall find his comfort in distress
All his life long, his rest in weariness."
The fire burned low; the laughter died away;
In night's long peace the little haven lay;
Under the stars' dead immortality
Two brief lives dreamed of love that should not die.
  The birds were singing gay from bough to bough,
Rock-thrush and wren and blackbird. From the brow
Of Drios streamed the silver mists of morn,
As the sun glittered on a world new-born.
Then Theseus, still half in a happy dream,
Thirsting arose and sought the murmuring stream
With Ariadne. From a rock it burst,
With a rock-hewn shrine beside, where men athirst

Worshipped the nymphs; above, three poplars swayed
And, underneath, the laughing brooklet played
With its bright pebbles and shook on either side
Its rushes, babbling to itself, and died,
Its brief race run, within the bitter sea.
But Laelaps bayed. Beneath a poplar-tree
A still shape lay, face downward, as in sleep.
Then Theseus paled, and seized one shoulder. Deep
In Aegle's heart her father's dagger lay.
He looked at Ariadne; then away,
With face flushed red. "No need" she cried "to tell!
I see it all, too late. I see, too well.
A new death lies between us? And last night
You let her misery watch our new delight!
O pitiless!" Above the white face there,
With the bright dew bejewelling its dark hair,
He laid his cloak; while by that chattering brook
Suddenly she recalled—so like its look—
That other stream where but two days ago
She sat with Phaedra—ah how full of woe
Had seemed that day—how happy now it seemed,
To this! She heard, dimly, as if she dreamed,
Theseus say "Come!" Together up the hill
They climbed, not knowing whither some blind will
Goaded them onward; till, hard-breathing, high
On its green top they stood. Windless the sky,

Waveless the sea they saw beneath them smile
Round Syros and sacred Delos and many an isle;
While up to heaven curled, behind the hill,
The smoke of the Naxians' city, straight and still.
She said "Did you love her, Theseus?" "Ah," he cried
"Can you not guess? We thought we should have died
Within two days or three; and, sharing death,
Should we not share those last brief hours of breath?
I loved her? Yes, I loved her. For three days
We were windbound in that isle—ah, passion plays
Strange tricks on us! I was so happy there
In the face of death and horror and despair,
And now, in the face of life and love and you,
So wretched; seeing myself faithless, untrue,
And all my life a wilderness of lies,
And all my hopes a whirl of mockeries.
Last night, O love, I told you how I came
To Athens, seeking honour, finding shame—
My father no proud king, but weak, oppressed,
False to my mother, murderer of his guest
('False to my mother!'—am I better now?),
And Athens full of faint hearts, fain to bow
To conquerors and robbers. Blind with rage
And bitterness at such a heritage
I sailed for Crete. And then a little while
In her kind arms I dreamed the world not vile,

And felt, poor idiot, though all else were vain,
Yet love at least could make life worth its pain.
And then I saw you—your eyes blinded me,
There in the face of death I would not see
That I, I too, was vile—Love too was vanity.
Yes, once I longed for ever to adore
Her face; last night, never to see it more.
It is time for truth. Now, now at last, I know
The gods have given us life to undergo;
Not to enjoy. Ah, bitter is their drink!
And yet what help? The best is not to shrink
But to be bold, to smile at what they give—
To know, to bear, to experience, to live.
Moments there may be, when our sufferings cease,
Moments of happiness, moments of peace.
From now I ask no more—Ah love, do you?
Do you find me changed; and these, rough words
    to woo?
Can you forgive me for this second death?
Can we make less bitter, side by side, life's breath?
I have done with oaths. I swear no constancy—
Yet, love, I love you. Can you still love me?"
Slowly she answered, and her voice rang cold,
"Can I 'forgive'? What meaning does it hold?
'Forgive you?'—would I punish?—no, not I.
Can I forget? Ah no, not till I die,

That still, cold face. Yet it is not the past
That stands between us; but the shadow cast
From it across the future. Better part
In tears to-day, than poisoned at the heart
Hereafter. For, though *you* may fling away
Love as a lie, life as a game to play,
Theseus, I cannot. Listen to my dream—
It is but truth. Beside the Hebrus stream
My mother's father ruled no famous race,
A little land. Yet happy, for the space
Of many a summer, with his queen he dwelt,
His people's shepherd. But when now they felt
Their years grow heavy, with the thaw of spring
Through the passes of Pangaeus, harrying
The Agrianians came. And ere his folk
Across the hills could rally to the smoke,
They drew their leaguer round his royal tower
In the city of Zyrine. Still his power
Might have laughed at sword and famine; but one eve
An Agrianian lured a girl to leave
The tower, with gifts—she gave herself that night
In love to him (ah me!), and with the light
By stealth they tracked her climbing home, and slew
The sleeping guards. Then when my grandsire knew
That all was lost and heard them storm the stair,
Upon their marriage-bed, at her own prayer,

133

He slew his queen, and over her was slain.
And so my mother, yet a babe, for gain
Was sold far south to Cnossus, there to be
The handmaid of the Queen Pasiphae,
The love of Minos. But which love think you
That I would choose?—the love my mother knew
In that proud palace, where I have seen her wet
With choking tears her purple coverlet;
Or the love of my mother's mother, loving one,
And dying with him, when the tale was done?
Was that a fancy? What can man ask more
Than love like hers to live and perish for?"
Under a fig they sat; and as she spoke,
Sadly with idle, listless hands she broke
The young buds, one by one, and let them rain
Betwixt her fingers; thinking how in vain
They, like her love, had gladdened with the spring.
But Theseus' voice rang sharp with suffering—
"Will you leave me, Ariadne? I know well
No man could blame you. Yet because I tell
The truth, not lovers' lies—the truth, though late,
Too late, I know—must our love turn to hate?
Ah come, my love, to Athens. Be my queen—
Forgive the memory of what has been.
I will strive to love no other from this day.
Do you believe me? More what man can say?

What though I might love others?—in the end
Can you not see that you, both wife and friend,
Hold me as sure as aught in life can be?
So others do. Years hence, when round your knee
Our tall sons gather, 'mid our people's praise,
Will you regret we severed not our ways?
O love, you love me. Lie not to your soul.
Have done with fancies. Ours to see things whole,
However sad. Better the clear grey eyes
Of Pallas, O my dear one, than the lies
Of Aphrodite. There, past Sunium,
The city of Pallas waits its mistress. Come!"
Pale she had grown and her voice faltered low—
"I cannot, Theseus, cannot. I must go.
Our dream is done—too much a dream it was,
Sweet as a dream, swift as a dream to pass.
Now it is fled, I will not stay behind
Clutching its memory. Lest in my mind
Even the memory grow soiled and base,
And I should come to hate that once loved face—
The loveliest still in all the world to me.
Theseus, there dwells a different deity
In my far country—He that brings to birth
Wild visions that transform this common earth.
His feet tread not alone the purple vine,
His feet are set on that far purple line

That crowns the hills of sunset; His the call
That makes men rise and follow till they fall.
And I—I seek, though loud the world laugh scorn,
The love I dream, the heart that for mine was born.
Nine times though visions cheat, the tenth comes true.
I care not though I search the wide world through—
You smile. You think me dream-sick. You are wise,
Your twenty years have taught you to despise
Such follies. You are man—your father's son,
Light weighs with men the heart they once have won.
But I am my mother's daughter; and women's worth
Shines prouder in the clear eyes of the North
Than in this false dark South—(O eyes so fair
Your mother gave, why lurks your father there?)
In my own land our Thracian maids love free
(How choose a mate in blind virginity?);
But once our hearts are given, we hold it base,
And childish, still to rove from face to face.
I will not bear—no, not to be a queen,
Your queen, my Theseus—those things I have seen
My mother suffer. Now our two ways part—
Ah, you will find you some less stubborn heart!
And yet beware!—women will love you well,
Who are so fair, so brave, so lovable;
And yet, O Theseus, he that dares to break
The hearts of others, in the end may wake

In grey old age, like Aegeus, weak, alone,
To find his own heart broke, or turned to stone,
And long for one with, in her fading eyes
Not youth, but all a life's dear memories."
She had risen to her feet. "Ah, you are hard,
Dear heart," he said. "And yet—we might have marred
What was so sweet—maybe 'tis better so.
Then best at once! Yet whither will you go?"
"In the Naxians' city, there behind the hill
I will find a ship—and then where Fortune will;
Whether to my own land, to seek the place
Across wild Rhodope, whence sprang my race—
The land of Orpheus and Eurydice
(O love, my love!)—or to the Friendless Sea,
To unknown shores and ways of men unknown,
Past golden Troy, where in the waste alone
Round Themiscyra (so the rumour runs)
To march against the West muster the Amazons.
Who knows? To dull this aching in my side,
I must go onward—and the world is wide.
How mad you think me, Theseus!"—(sad she smiled)
"Wilful and blind and wanton as a child—
Ah, if men ask you of your princess, say
Wild Dionysus whirled her far away,
The bride of fantasy; and on this head
You would have crowned in Athens, set instead

A wayward wanderer's crown of erring stars.
Farewell, my Theseus. In new loves and wars
That heart will heal, those eyes no more be wet—
Do not too much remember; nor too much forget."
So passionately they clung as if to part
Were death itself; until almost her heart
Failed and she moaned "Ah, better might it be
To have you false than another true to me?"
"Then stay!" he cried. She had never seemed so fair,
That fearless face, that tossing golden hair.
But from his arms she slipped; with one last look
She gazed at him, and then with lips that shook
Turned down the hill. Far off he watched her go,
With Laelaps bounding round her, sad and slow,
Like Artemis, through glens of Pholoe
Roving in tameless, bright virginity.
Then to the beach he turned, with eyes so sad
That none dared question him; and there he bad
Burn Aegle's body by the cold sea-wave.
So, on the headland, high they heaped her grave
And with the next red dawn put forth to sea.
In the black sail the breeze piped merrily,
While Sunium and Aegina and Troezene
Rose round him changeless, as if nought had been.
But them he saw not; nor, hand clasped in hand,
Those lovers round him watching their dear land

Smile, all undreamed of, on their eyes once more,
Glad with the vision of long years in store
Of happiness together; but to him
They and the Attic hills alike were dim,
For still he saw her down the mountain-track
Departing—and not even looking back
(Perhaps she could not bear to?) in farewell.
Then as, past Sunium, the citadel
Of Athens gleamed, he thought of Aegle's face,
Of her last song—how Fate gave her the grace
She craved for; since she had known Love at last
Ere Death, though Death had followed Love so fast;
He thought how true her love, what might have been,
Had but a lovelier never come between;
How deep she slumbered now, and Euthycles,
Laid in strange lands, yet lost in dreamless ease
That yearned no more for home. "Ah God, that I"
He groaned "had died, too, in my victory!"
So as he sat and brooded on the past,
He took no thought how still upon the mast
The black sail hung; till lo! the sudden roar
Of the keel on the shingle of Phalerum shore.
A few sad fishers watched; then one espied
The captives' waving hands, and madly cried
To all the rest, and high in air they threw
Their pointed caps and thronged about the crew

139

With stammering questions, while two turned to run
Headlong towards Athens through the burning sun.
As he had dreamed with Aegle, while they lay
That even on the islet, so to-day
All came to pass. But Aegle was not there.
For as they walked, suddenly through the glare
Of that white afternoon there burst a shout
And from the gateway stormed in headlong rout
The men of Athens, like a swarming hive,
Laughing and shouting to see their dead alive.
They brought a chariot. Up the ringing street,
With flowers in showers before his horses' feet,
Prince Theseus passed; by Victory's wreath-hung shrine
To the grey palace of Erechtheus' line.
But there no Aegeus stood. And Theseus thought
"To him, if not to me, this day has brought
Some joy at least—O quick—let him be found!"
Through the tall door he strode and gazed around—
Where once Medea's tapestries had thrown
Their eastern splendour, all lay bleak and lone.
But a shepherd-lad came running, and whispered fast
In Theseus' ear—with hurrying steps they passed
To the sheer rampart of Athene's hill.
On the rocks below something lay white and still—
Aegeus the King. "Yonder" the young lad said
"Upon the Muses' Hill I sat and fed

My sheep, till suddenly the shouts began.
I looked—there lay the Black Ship—and here ran,
Stumbling, the King and leant against the wall.
Seaward he looked—and then I saw him fall."
They sought his side—with calm, unruffled brow
The old King lay. Said Theseus "Leave me now";
Then gazing on that dead face, bitterly
He whispered "Father, were you not to see
This one last happiness? Or is the end
Of life a blessing nought else need amend?
Dead lies King Minos too beyond the sea—
Your strife is ended in eternity.
At last, though life denies, death grants us rest."
With heart too full to weep, towards the west
He looked, to the Isthmus; thinking how he came
Across those hills, athirst for life and fame,
And found both bitter. Then beneath him there
He saw the plain of Athens, spreading fair
With corn and olive to the guardian sea;
He heard the buzzing throng expectantly
Waiting, far off, the coming of their King;
Till his heart rose above its suffering
And he thought "There is this to live for. These
    remain—
This people. I have gained but grief and pain,
Yet the Cretan yoke is broken. All has not been in vain.

141

And this is little to what shall be done,
When this torn land is welded into one,
When these wild hills of Attica become
One race, from Mount Parnes to Sunium,
With their eyes turned towards Athene's Hill.
So they shall live by happy hearths at will,
Though I cannot. If rest is not for me,
If all my life and love prove but a sea
Of storm and homelessness, so be it then!
Short at the longest are the lives of men,
Till I too, father, find my last long rest."
Stooping he crossed the hands upon the breast
And closed the eyes that looked a last time now
Towards far Troezene, and kissed that quiet brow,
Then passed the gate; while loud and louder broke
The storm of happy shouting, till it woke
Echo on echo and wavering died away.
But in the stillness of Phalerum bay,
Far off, from hull to masthead blazing free,
A black ship slowly drifted out to sea.
Like a long snake its smoke-cloud drifted slow
Past Salamis, past Aegina, till the glow,
There where the setting sun blazed fieriest,
Vanished. Past Corinth paled the crimson west,
Into her arms Night gathered the last flushed
     mountain-crest.

ENVOI

Love, this is all. No need to tell
The sadder end you know too well—
How Ariadne's heart guessed true
And Theseus changed old loves for new,
Till with the lover that played so free
With Love, Love too played bitterly—
How for the lure of Phaedra's face,
For Helen in her girlhood's grace,
He saw his own son go to die,
His mother to captivity;
Till Athens flung him from his throne
To death in exile, old, alone.
Yet his own youth's dream came true no
    less.
His work endured. Men learnt to bless
The memory of him whose hand
First forged in one the Attic land;
Who rose again with shadowy sword
To hew a path through the Persian horde,
A spectre grey in the summer sun
By the red marsh of Marathon.
   But Ariadne?—none may guess
The long road of her loneliness;
None knows if Dionysus gave
The love she dreamed, or a dreamless grave.

Only her memory lives, her crown
Of errant stars still glitters down
With the cold Heavens' immortal fire
On the mortal flame of man's desire,
Will glitter still, dear heart, when we
Are ashes of eternity,
And what you whispered long ago
Time has hidden where none shall know.
Our world will fade like hers—no less
Women will still stake happiness,
Honour, and life, for a face that stirs
Their hearts with the same wild pulse as
    hers,
And loving vainly—yet not in vain—
Go forth made rich with only pain.
For Love is deathless and yet, alas,
Loves fade faster than summer grass;
Even the heart that's faithfullest
Sleeps at last on a colder breast.
And yet no matter, though forgot,
So life's long pageant perish not—
If of the fair and the brave that fell,
Sometimes is left a tale to tell.

For EU product safety concerns, contact us at Calle de José Abascal, 56–1°,
28003 Madrid, Spain or eugpsr@cambridge.org.

www.ingramcontent.com/pod-product-compliance
Ingram Content Group UK Ltd.
Pitfield, Milton Keynes, MK11 3LW, UK
UKHW010048140625
459647UK00012BB/1689